D0436824

A HISTORICAL READER

Native American
Perspectives

Printed in the United States of America

ISBN 0-618-04820-0

1 2 3 4 5 6 7 — QKT — 06 05 04 03 02 01 00

Table of Contents

970
Na

PART II: RELIGION

*Throughout the reader, vocabulary words appear in boldface
type and are footnoted. Specialized or technical words and phrases
appear in lightface type and are footnoted.*

Prophecy
and Contact

Prophecies of Our Grandparents

BY A STORYTELLER (ZUNI)
Translated by Alvina Quam

Native American tribes have strong oral traditions. They pass their histories from one generation to the next through spoken stories. The most important events described in these stories usually contain some underlying meaning, or prophecy, that often describes or predicts a future event. More specifically, these oral traditions often include prophecies that not only predict the arrival of non-Indians but the consequences of establishing contact with these unfamiliar people. Although some of these narratives may actually have been passed down after the arrival of the white man, nonetheless, they relate Indian values and worldview. The following is a prophecy told among the Zuni Indians of western New Mexico, one of several tribes that make up the Pueblo culture.

Many years ago when our grandparents foresaw what our future would be like, they spoke their prophecies among themselves and passed them on to the children before them.

"Cities will progress and then decay to the ways of the lowest beings. Drinkers of dark liquids[1] will come upon the land, speaking nonsense and filth. Then the end shall be nearer.

"Population will increase until the land can hold no more. The tribes of men will mix. The dark liquids they drink will cause the people to fight among themselves. Families will break up: father against children and the children against one another.

"Maybe when the people have outdone themselves, then maybe, the stars will fall upon the land, or drops of hot water will rain upon the earth. Or the land will turn under. Or our father, the sun, will not rise to start the day. Then our possessions will turn into beasts and devour us whole.

"If not, there will be an odor from gases, which will fill the air we breathe, and the end for us shall come.

"But the people themselves will bring upon themselves what they receive. From what has resulted, time alone will tell what the future holds for us."

---

[1] Drinkers of dark liquids—European whites who consumed alcoholic drinks. Alcohol, which has had a terrible impact on many Native American societies, was virtually unknown to the Indians of eastern North America until the arrival of Europeans.

QUESTIONS TO CONSIDER

1. What will the "dark liquids" cause people to do?

2. What will be the cause of the disasters predicted for the future?

3. What, in your opinion, does this prophecy reveal about the Zuni view of their history?

The Arrival of the White Men

TRADITIONAL LEGENDS (MICMAC, CHINOOK)

When Native Americans and Europeans first encountered one another, their vocabularies usually lacked words to accurately describe each other's appearance, clothing, equipment, language, skills, tools, and even behavior. Thus, in their first accounts of contact between Indians and whites, each used their own terms and ideas to describe things they had never seen before and did not completely comprehend. The first of these two contact accounts comes from the Micmac Indians living along the Atlantic coast of Canada. The second story comes from the Pacific coast of North America and is told by the Chinook Indians settled along the Columbia River in what is now Washington state. The Micmacs first encountered Europeans in the early 1600s, whereas the Chinooks first saw white men in the mid to late 1700s. Even though the Chinooks and Micmacs lived nearly 3,000 miles apart and the Micmac story may be as much as 100 years older, their descriptions of initial encounters with whites have strong similarities.

The Dream of the White Robe and the Floating Island: A Micmac Legend

When there were no people in this country but Indians, before white people were known, a young woman had a strange dream. She dreamed that a small island came floating in toward the land. On the island were tall trees and living beings. Among them was a man dressed in garments made of rabbit skins.

In those days it was the custom, when anyone had an unusual dream, to consult the wise men of the tribe, especially the prophets and magicians.[1] So the girl related her dream and asked what it meant. The wise men pondered but could make nothing of it. On the second day after the girl's dream, however, something happened that explained it.

When they got up that morning, they saw what seemed to be a small island that had drifted near to the land and become fixed there. There were trees on the island, and what seemed to be a number of bears were crawling about on the branches.

All the Micmac[2] men seized their bows and arrows and spears and rushed down to the shore to shoot the bears. But they stopped in surprise when they saw that the creatures were not bears but men.[3] And what had seemed to be a small island with trees was really a large boat with long poles rising above it. While the Indians stood watching, some of the men on the ship lowered a strangely built canoe into the water. Several of them jumped into it and paddled ashore.

---

[1] prophets and magicians—important figures in Indian life, often called shamans, they are responsible for the physical health as well as the spiritual well-being of the people.

[2] Micmac—Native people that originally inhabited what is now the Canadian province of Nova Scotia.

[3] The Micmac may have initially thought the Europeans were bears because they wore fur clothing and had beards, which Native men rarely did.

Among those in the strange canoe was a man dressed in white.[4] As he came toward the shore, he made signs of friendship, by raising his hand toward heaven. He talked to the Indians in an earnest manner, in a language they did not understand.[5]

Now people began to question the girl about her dream.

"Was it an island like this that you saw in your dream?"

"Yes."

"Is the man in the white robe the one you saw in your dream?"

"Yes, he was."

Then some of the prophets and magicians were greatly displeased—displeased because the coming of these strangers to their land had been revealed to a young girl instead of to them. If an enemy had been about to make an attack upon them, they could have foreseen it and foretold it by the power of their magic. But of the coming of this white-robed man, who proved to be a priest of a new religion, they knew nothing.

The new teacher gradually won his way into their favor, though the magicians opposed him. The people received his instruction and were baptized. The priest learned their language and gave them the prayer book written in ornamental mark-writing.[6]

---

[4] man dressed in white—French Catholic priest. The French attempted to convert the Indians they encountered to Catholic Christianity.

[5] a language they did not understand—French. The first Europeans to establish contact with the Micmacs were from France.

[6] ornamental mark-writing—written language. When the Europeans arrived in North America, Indians did not have a written language.

The First Ship: A Chinook Legend
Reported by Franz Boas

An old woman in a Clatsop village near the mouth of Big River[7] mourned the death of her son. For a year she grieved. One day she stopped her crying and took a walk along the beach where she had often gone in happier days.

As she was returning to the village, she saw a strange something out in the water not far from shore. At first she thought it was a whale. When she came nearer, she saw two spruce trees standing upright on it.

"It's not a whale," she said to herself, "it's a monster."

When she came near the strange thing that lay at the edge of the water, she saw that its outside was covered with copper and that ropes were tied to the spruce trees. Then a bear came out of the strange thing and stood on it. It looked like a bear, but the face was the face of a human being.

"Oh, my son is dead," she wailed, "and now the thing we have heard about is on our shore."

Weeping, the old woman returned to her village. People who heard her called to others, "An old woman is crying. Someone must have struck her."

The men picked up their bows and arrows and rushed out to see what was the matter.

"Listen!" an old man said.

They heard the woman wailing, "Oh, my son is dead, and the thing we have heard about is on our shore."

All the people ran to meet her. "What is it? Where is it?" they asked.

"Ah, the thing we have heard about in tales is lying over there." She pointed toward the south shore of the

---

[7] Big River—the Columbia River in what is now the state of Washington. The Clatsop village was near where the river flows into the Pacific Ocean.

village. "There are two bears on it, or maybe they are people."

Then the Indians ran toward the thing that lay near the edge of the water. The two creatures on it held copper kettles in their hands. When the Clatsop arrived at the beach, the creatures put their hands to their mouths and asked for water.

Two of the Indians ran inland, hid behind a log awhile, and then ran back to the beach. One of them climbed up on the strange thing, entered it, and looked around inside. It was full of boxes, and he found long strings of brass buttons.

When he went outside to call his relatives to see the inside of the thing, he found that they had already set fire to it. He jumped down and joined the two creatures and the Indians on shore.

The strange thing burned just like fat. Everything burned except the iron, the copper, and the brass. Then the Clatsop took the two strange-looking men to their chief.

"I want to keep one of the men with me," said the chief.

Soon the people north of the river heard about the strange men and the strange thing, and they came to the Clatsop village. The Willapa came from across the river, the Chehalis and the Cowlitz from farther north, and even the Quinault from up the coast. And people from up the river came also—the Klickitat and others farther up.[8]

The Clatsop sold the iron, brass, and copper. They traded one nail for a good deerskin. For a long necklace of shells they gave several nails. One man traded a piece of brass two fingers wide for a slave.

None of the Indians had ever seen iron or brass before. The Clatsop became rich selling the metal to other tribes.

---

[8] The Willapa, Chehalis, Cowlitz, Quinault, and Klickitat were tribes that lived in what is now Washington state near the Pacific coast and the Columbia River.

The two Clatsop chiefs kept the two men who came on the ship. One stayed at the village called Clatsop, and the other stayed at the village on the cape.

QUESTIONS TO CONSIDER

1. What do the words used to describe unfamiliar things say about the Micmac and Clatsop ways of life?

2. What are the similarities and differences in the ways that the Micmacs and the Chinooks described the Europeans?

3. How are the Europeans viewed in these accounts?

4. Why, in your opinion, is Native-American history often passed from generation to generation in the form of prophecy?

A Cheyenne Memory

BY JOHN STANDS IN TIMBER (CHEYENNE)

Sometimes the first contact between Indian and white cultures did not come in the form of face-to-face meetings. Often Native Americans were familiar with European trade goods, tools, and diseases long before they encountered their first European. This is also true of the horse, an animal first brought from Europe to North America in the 1500s. By the mid-1600s, horses from Spanish settlements in Mexico had returned to the wild, had migrated, or had been sold by Indian traders northward onto the Great Plains. By the late 1700s, the Indian people east of the Missouri River were highly skilled at capturing and using horses for hunting and warfare. The Cheyenne were one of many tribes whose way of life changed dramatically through the use of the horse.

The first Cheyenne[1] who ever saw horses saw them come in to water at a lake, down in the country that is now Wyoming. He went down closer to look, and then he thought of the prophecy of Sweet Medicine,[2] that there would be animals with round hoofs and shaggy manes and tails, and men could ride on their backs into the Blue Vision.[3] He went back to the village and told the old Indians, and they remembered.

So they fixed a snare, and when a horse stepped into it they ran to him and tied him down. Then they got a rawhide rope on him and all hung onto it, and they got him broken that way. The prophecy had been that they were to ride on his back, so after he was tame enough to follow a person on a rope they tried it, and got along all right. They used him then to find and catch others. The stream that empties into the North Platte River there they named Horse River or Horse Creek and that was where the 1851 Treaty[4] was signed by so many tribes of Indians with the United States.

They said the first horse they got was blue colored and the second was a buckskin. It was before the tribe divided, but already some Cheyennes were traveling and hunting on the southern Plains.

After they got the first horses they learned there were more of them in the South and they went there

---

[1] Cheyenne—a people who migrated from Minnesota through the Dakotas and finally onto the Great Plains. In the late 1700s, the Cheyenne adopted the use of the horse for hunting and warfare and became a nomadic people. By the early 1800s, they were divided into two groups: the Northern Cheyenne inhabited an area along the North Platte River in what is now western Nebraska, while the Southern Cheyenne lived along the upper Arkansas River in western Kansas.

[2] Sweet Medicine—a shaman or spiritual leader of the Cheyenne tribe.

[3] Blue Vision—the blue outline of the distant Rocky Mountains seen on the western horizon from the flat landscape of the Great Plains.

[4] 1851 Treaty—agreement to remain within new tribal boundaries and not to attack white settlers heading westward across the plains.

after them. That was when they began the religion called the Horse Worship.[5] Later, when the white men came and brought bigger horses, the Cheyennes began calling their own smaller ones Indian horses and the others white man's horses, to show the difference.

---

[5] Horse Worship—The horse became an important symbol of honor and status in Plains Indian societies. The use of horses allowed the Indians to hunt buffalo in larger numbers and increase the food supply for their people, which in turn led to a growth in population. Among the Cheyenne people the process of capturing, training, and using horses took on a strong spiritual significance.

QUESTIONS TO CONSIDER

1. Why were horses so important to the Cheyenne people?

2. Where did the Cheyenne find these horses?

3. What does "A Cheyenne Memory" reveal about the role of horses in Cheyenne culture?

My Sun Is Set

ANONYMOUS

The grim prophecies of many Native people came true when white settlers began to move westward. The sad fulfillment of these visions is captured in this elegy, or song of mourning, written by an unknown tribal elder. Based on references he makes, the anonymous author would appear to be a Plains Indian, possibly writing sometime in the first half of the nineteenth century, when white soldiers and their weapons had begun to appear on the frontier and overhunting was starting to destroy the buffalo herds.

My sun is set. My day is done. Darkness is stealing over me. Before I lie down to rise no more I will speak to my people. Hear me, for this is not the time to tell a lie. The Great Spirit made us, and gave us this land we live in. He gave us the buffalo, antelope, and deer for food and clothing. Our hunting grounds stretched from the Mississippi to the great mountains.[1] We were free as the winds and heard no man's commands. We fought our enemies, and feasted our friends. Our

---

[1] the great mountains—probably the Rocky Mountains of the American and Canadian West.

braves drove away all who would take our game. They captured women and horses from our foes. Our children were many and our herds were large. Our old men talked with spirits and made good medicine. Our young men hunted and made love to the girls. Where the **tipi**[2] was, there we stayed, and no house imprisoned us. No one said, "To this line is my land, to that is yours." Then the white man came to our hunting grounds, a stranger. We gave him meat and presents, and told him [to] go in peace. He looked on our women and stayed to live in our tipis. His fellows came to build their roads across our hunting grounds. He brought among us the mysterious iron that shoots.[3] He brought with him the magic water that makes men foolish.[4] With his trinkets and beads he even bought the girl I loved. I said, "The white man is not a friend, let us kill him." But their numbers were greater than blades of grass. They took away the buffalo and shot down our best warriors. They took away our lands and surrounded us by fences. Their soldiers camped outside with cannon to shoot us down. They wiped the trails of our people from the face of the prairies. They forced our children to forsake the ways of their fathers. When I turn to the east I see no dawn. When I turn to the west the approaching night hides all.

---

[2] **tipi**—tent used by Plains Indians, sometimes spelled "tepee" or "teepee."

[3] mysterious iron that shoots—rifle.

[4] magic water that makes men foolish—liquor.

QUESTIONS TO CONSIDER

1. Why has the author apparently given up all hope for the survival of Native people and their culture?

2. What does the author mean when he says that whites "wiped the trails of our people from the face of the prairies"?

Ways of Life

This Inuit mother and her child were photographed in Alaska in 1903. At the time, Inuit contact with whites in Alaska was mainly with miners and explorers seeking a Northwest Passage from Europe to the Pacific. The Inuit people, sometimes known as Eskimos, live in a land dominated by the cold and the continual threat of starvation.

Apaches A Jicarilla Apache brave and his squaw pose in ceremonial clothes for a photograph in 1874. The Jicarilla Apaches are among several Apache groups that live in northern New Mexico. ▶

Pueblo girls Photographer Edward Curtis captures two Tewa girls wearing traditional dress as they beat a rug outside their home in northern New Mexico. ▼

◀ **Brave Iroquois** French incursion into Iroquois territory in what is now New England and Quebec was halted when the Iroquois Nation joined forces with the British in 1754. The French and Indian War ended in 1763 with the signing of the Treaty of Paris, which stripped France of all its North American land claims.

◀ **Warrior of Florida** Among the many tribes encountered by British, French, and Spanish explorers were the Seminole tribes of Florida.

While the most well-known type of Native American home is the tipi, such homes were favored only by nomadic tribes like those that roamed the Great Plains. Other tribes built their homes from mud bricks, clay, or wood. Many settled into permanent towns and villages, some of which survive today.

Background Piegan tipis.

Pima Ki A family residence in the southwest. ▶

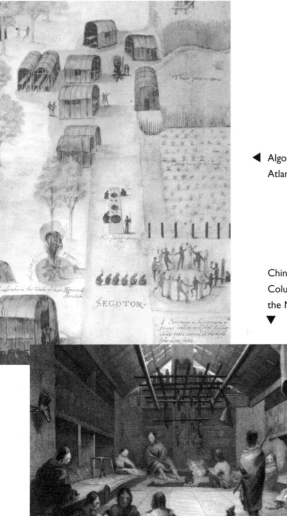

◀ Algonquian village on the Atlantic coast.

Chinook lodge in the Columbia River valley of the Northwest.
▼

▲

Plains tribes such as the Cheyenne and Sioux hunt buffalo for both food and shelter. After the introduction of the horse to North America, Native Americans hunted buffalo on horseback. The buffalo were hunted nearly to extinction by white settlers moving west.

Native Americans hunt deer in Florida by disguising themselves in deerskins.

▼

Three men gather rice in a canoe in the Great Lakes.
▼

Native Americans guard their cornfields from birds and other animals. Corn was introduced by Native Americans to white settlers when they first arrived in the New World.

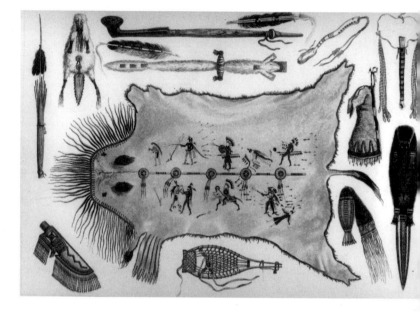

▲

Everyday items used by Plains Indians in the early 1840s.

Baskets Hopi baskets crafted by women. ▶

This Sioux scalp shirt is made of hide and decorated with beading, eagle feathers, and human hair. It was not only a shirt but also a trophy attesting to the wearer's standing as a warrior.
▼

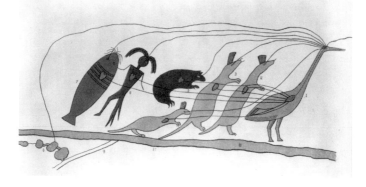

▲

This pictograph shows the "signatures" of Chippewa chiefs from Wisconsin, presented in Washington as a petition on behalf of their people on January 28, 1849.

▲

Native Americans in Florida cook fish and game over a barbecue in 1591.

Religion

The Code of Handsome Lake

BY CHIEF JACOB THOMAS (CAYUGA)

The American Revolution cost the Iroquois people their land and their independence. By the 1790s, the Iroquois faced a bleak future. Handsome Lake, the founder of the Iroquois Longhouse religion described in this selection, was the half-brother of Cornplanter, a Seneca chief who had been influenced by Christian teachings. In 1799, after Handsome Lake had nearly died from alcohol abuse and illness, he recovered his health and spread his newly found hope for an Iroquois revival. Handsome Lake's message incorporated traditional Iroquois beliefs and rituals with an insistence that his followers abstain from alcohol, repent for their misdeeds, and practice proper family behavior. The Longhouse religion continues to this day among the Iroquois people. Chief Jacob Thomas, a current leader of the Cayuga tribe of the Iroquois nation and a Longhouse follower, presents his own retelling of Handsome Lake's story.

Towards the end of the 1700s, the Iroquois Confederacy[1] began to deteriorate. Although the Confederacy had protected their territory from the Dutch, English, French, and the Thirteen Colonies (which later became the United States of America), their population was down to one-quarter of what it had been when white people had first arrived. Diseases to which they had no immunity—like measles, chicken pox, and smallpox—had swept through their villages. In 1779 the American General John Sullivan destroyed the basis of Iroquois power by burning their villages and cornfields and destroying a large number of the warehouses that held their food supplies.[2] The Hotinónshon:ni[3] saw their territories decreasing and many of them turned to the fur trade for survival.

In those days, many people would gather after the harvest and at this meeting a leader would decide when it was time for the men to go to their winter hunting places. After they had set a time, the men and their leader would prepare their canoes. Then they would take half the harvest and leave the other half for the people who remained in the village. When they arrived at their hunting place, they took great care to store their canoes, making them safe, so that the ice on the river would not damage them. They would walk into the woods and make camp, for they knew what to expect from the winter there. The men were very fortunate that the winter hunting and trapping often brought great bounty. The leader, who always watched the weather, would send a runner

---

[1] Iroquois Confederacy—union of the six Iroquois tribes (Cayuga, Oneida, Onondaga, Mohawk, Seneca, and Tuscarora) that until the American Revolution made up the most powerful Native American diplomatic and military force in North America.

[2] In 1779, under orders from General George Washington, Sullivan's army destroyed more than forty Indian villages in upstate New York and ended the influence of the Iroquois Confederacy.

[3] Hotinónshon:ni—the name the Iroquois people call themselves. It literally means "people of the longhouse."

to check the river. When the ice on the river went down and it was safe to travel, the hunters would prepare to leave, putting all their game into the canoes and heading to a settlement called Pittsburgh in what is now Pennsylvania.

Once they arrived in Pittsburgh, the first thing they did was trade furs for kegs of rum and whiskey. As they started on their journey home, they would start drinking. They tied their canoes together, making a raft or barge, so that they continued to paddle together, but they would get so drunk that some of them would fall out of their canoes and drown. This would go on until they reached their village. Meanwhile, the people who remained in the village would hear their hunters returning from trading the hides and would gather all the children and run down to the shore, meet the canoes, and help them unload the whiskey and rum.

For a number of days a huge party would take place until all the alcohol was gone. Sometimes some of the people would run away into the woods, returning to the village days later only to find bodies lying here and there. Some of the people would be hurt, some would be passed out, others would have been killed during the course of the drinking. When this was all over, the people would bury the dead, clean up, and try to start over.

Sganyadaí:yoh (Handsome Lake) was a member of the Seneca Nation who lived during this time. He had been born in 1735 in the Seneca village of Ganawágas on the Genesee River.[4] He held a Seneca **sachem**[5] for his people. As sachem, he represented the honorable position of leadership of his nation.

---

[4] Genesee River—a river that flows through western New York state and empties into Lake Ontario.

[5] **sachem**—title given to a leader or tribal chief.

Sganyadaí:yoh was a heavy drinker, one of alcohol's many victims, and his people saw their leader's suffering. His daughter took care of him so he could rest and recover from his illness. He was sick for a period of four years and had to be confined to his bed.

During a time when he was feeling better than usual, he began thinking of his position as chief in the Confederacy—and then he thought about the way he had been carrying on. Many times as he lay there, he looked up through the smoke hole in the roof to the outside. Seeing the top of the trees and the stars in the sky, he started to think and asked himself, "Where did all this come from? Why is this all here? What am I doing here? What does this all mean?"

Sganyadaí:yoh started remembering all the things that he had heard since he was a young boy. How some day the white's firewater[6] would destroy all of them. He began to remember who he was and what his relationship was to Shongwàyadíhs:on (the Creator—literally, "He who made you"), so each morning he started to give thanks for having seen another day. As he lay there looking through the smoke hole, he thought, "Maybe this lifestyle I have been living is wrong, is not getting me or my people anywhere."

Every time Sganyadaí:yoh started thinking good thoughts, he began to feel better. And as he started to feel better, his strength returned. He lay in bed for four years and started to think more clearly about who he was and why he was here. As he started to recover and gain strength, he gave thanks.

Now he realized he had to make a decision, that he had better quit [drinking] for good and start thinking of his people, his relationship with Shongwàyadíhs:on and how his nation would survive.

---

[6] firewater—liquor or alcohol.

One June morning, as the dew was beginning to dry, Sganyadaí:yoh awoke. His daughter and her husband, sitting outside by the doorway cleaning beans for planting, heard him stir. His daughter turned to look at the door and saw her father standing at the doorway. When he collapsed, she was so frightened that she yelled to her husband, "Go and tell my uncle Cornplanter (Gayentwágeh) that his brother looks like he has passed away." So her husband rushed over to Cornplanter's, then to his nephew Black Snake. Cornplanter said, "As soon as I am finished covering the seeds, I will be over."

Black Snake was the first to arrive. He went straight to his uncle's bedside, examined him, and felt his chest. He felt a warm spot on his uncle's chest. The people were already assembled and had begun mourning, thinking that the great leader was gone. They started making burial arrangements, dressing Sganyadaí:yoh in his finest traditional clothes.

But Black Snake said, "Be patient, we will wait. Do not grieve." About mid-morning, the people suddenly noticed that the great leader had opened his eyes and was moving his lips. It was as if he had just awakened. Then Black Snake said to his uncle, "How are you?"

His uncle was not able to answer him. All he could do was move his lips. He was unable to say a word. Again it looked as if he went back to sleep.

It was just about noon when he began to move and open his eyes. Again Black Snake said to his uncle, "How are you feeling?" This time Sganyadaí:yoh was able to speak.

He told the gathering, "I saw some very bright sunlight with great colors, more brilliant than ever before. It was very good to be there. I heard a voice as I lay in bed. A man asked me to come outside. He called me a second time but I knew I couldn't move, for I had not moved in a long time. I tried to sit up, even though I knew that

I couldn't. But I found that I was able to stand and walk and step outside.

"Then I saw three men standing off a little way and one called to me. These men all looked the same. They were very beautiful, very handsome, their faces were painted. Each one carried a bow and arrows in one hand and elderberry branches in the other. I had never seen anyone look as they did. It seemed as if their feet were not touching the ground. They told me, 'Our feet never touch the ground.' They were sent to Earth by Shongwàyadíhs:on to look for a certain strongminded man who was doing wrong. This man had to repent for using obné:gab (alcohol).

"I said to them, 'I have been hoping, if it would be possible, to walk again on Earth. I repent that I sang the Ohgí:weh (the Death Chant or the Ghost Dance) songs. The quivering songs and dances have brought evil to my life and made me do wrong things.'

"Then the Three Messengers said, 'We think there are some other things that Shongwàyadíhs:on wants to hear.'

"I said, 'I am hoping the Great Spirit may let me walk again on Earth. I now repent of all the evil things I have done and I also repent of using alcohol, which made Shongwàyadíhs:on sad.'

"Then the messengers said to me, 'That is what He wanted to hear. So now He has heard it all. So He who created you has decided that He is going to give you strength and power. He will let you walk again on Earth. He has appointed you to do some important things for Him. So this is what will be done: There are two medicine people,[7] a man and a wife, among you who will prepare medicine for you. Their names are Ojiskwá:then and Gayengó:gwas. They will go into the woods early in the

---

[7] medicine people—Native American healers who tend to both the physical and spiritual needs of the people.

morning and pick the medicine. This native medicine will be prepared for you to drink for three days. If you are unable to use it up by the third morning, then the rest can be cast away. When they have made this medicine for you, then you will be isolated for three days.

"'The people shall pick strawberries early in the morning and make it into a strawberry drink. People shall assemble in the Longhouse[8] and the leaders shall appoint two men to serve the drink, and each person shall give thanksgiving. They shall not say that you are fortunate you recovered, but shall say that we are very fortunate you have recovered.' The messengers said, 'This will help you regain your strength.'

"Never let us hear your relations say, 'He is poor and fortunate to wálk again on Earth.' Whenever your relations mention this, they will say, 'We are fortunate he rose again and walked on Earth.'

"Your relations will assemble in the Longhouse tomorrow morning and then you will see them. The ceremony will begin at noontime. The ceremony will continue with the Great Dance, the Feather Dance. It is necessary to have the strawberry drink prepared because this is what we give thanks with. The strawberry drink will be served and each person will give thanks."

The people gathered and did as they were instructed. Many people were there, and when Sganyadaí:yoh approached them, some were sad. His daughter helped him as they prepared for the Great Feather Dance.

When it was over and everything that the messengers had requested was completed, he told the people of his vision. He said, "The messengers were sent by Shongwàyadíhs:on to tell the people on Earth that they were not aware of wrongdoing—and because the

---

[8] Longhouse—typical home of the Iroquois people, a wooden structure often sixty feet long in which several related families lived.

Creator had given thanksgiving and renewal to Sganyadaí:yoh after he repented of his wrongdoing, they had chosen him to be the one to bring the Good Message (or Gaiwí:yo) of Shongwàyadíhs:on (the Creator's highest code of ethics)."

QUESTIONS TO CONSIDER

1. What actions did Handsome Lake take while he was sick to make himself better? What are some things that he began to remember?

2. What did Handsome Lake believe that he had done wrong?

3. What did Handsome Lake order his people to do to give thanks?

4. What elements do you find in this account of the Longhouse religion that might provide spiritual comfort to the Iroquois people?

Cruelty at the San Miguel Mission

BY JANITIN (KAMIA)

*The treatment of Native people at colonial California's missions by
some Spanish and, later, Mexican Catholic priests has long been
controversial. Priests were expected to gain as many converts to
the Christian faith as they could and also to use Indian labor to
maximize the food and craft goods each mission produced. Janitin,
a Kamia, was captured sometime during the 1820s and brought
under guard to Mission San Miguel, south of San Diego near the
present-day border between the United States and Mexico. As an
old man in 1878, Janitin told an interviewer about the ordeal he
had undergone and displayed the scars he had received at the
hands of the Dominican priests. Cruelty was not always the case,
however. Some priests from another Catholic order, the Franciscans,
were welcomed by Native people because they were gentle and
shared the Indians' poverty and simplicity. That clearly was not
Janitin's experience.*

I and two of my relatives went down from the Sierra of Neji to the beach of el Rosarito,[1] to catch clams for eating and to carry to the sierra[2] as we were accustomed to do all the years; we did no harm to anyone on the road, and on the beach we thought of nothing more than catching and drying clams in order to carry them to our village.

While we were doing this, we saw two men on horseback coming rapidly towards us; my relatives were immediately afraid and they fled with all speed, hiding themselves in a very dense willow grove which then existed in the canyon of the Rancho del Rosarito.

As soon as I saw myself alone, I also became afraid of those men and ran to the forest in order to join my companions, but already it was too late, because in a moment they overtook me and lassoed and dragged me for a long distance, wounding me much with the branches over which they dragged me, pulling me lassoed as I was with their horses running; after this they roped me with my arms behind and carried me off to the Mission of San Miguel, making me travel almost at a run in order to keep up with their horses, and when I stopped a little to catch my wind, they lashed me with the lariats[3] that they carried, making me understand by signs that I should hurry; after much traveling in this manner, they diminished the pace and lashed me in order that I would always travel at the pace of the horses.

When we arrived at the mission, they locked me in a room for a week; the father [a Dominican priest] made me go to his **habitation**[4] and he talked to me by means of an interpreter, telling me that he would make me a

---

[1] Sierra of Neji to the beach of el Rosarito—the Neji Mountains, part of southern California's Coastal Range, to the beach of el Rosarito, a location on the Pacific Ocean near present-day San Diego.

[2] sierra—rugged range of mountains having a jagged profile.

[3] lariats—ropes for catching horses and cattle.

[4] **habitation**—home or room.

Christian, and he told me many things that I did not understand, and Cunnur, the interpreter, told me that I should do as the father told me, because now I was not going to be set free, and it would go very bad with me if I did not consent in it. They gave me *atole de mayz* [corn gruel] to eat which I did not like because I was not accustomed to that food; but there was nothing else to eat.

One day they threw water on my head and gave me salt to eat, and with this the interpreter told me that now I was Christian and that I was called *Jesús*: I knew nothing of this, and I tolerated it all because in the end I was a poor Indian and did not have **recourse**[5] but to conform myself and tolerate the things they did with me.

The following day after my baptism, they took me to work with the other Indians, and they put me to cleaning a *milpa* [cornfield] of maize; since I did not know how to manage the hoe that they gave me, after hoeing a little, I cut my foot and could not continue working with it, but I was put to pulling out the weeds by hand, and in this manner I did not finish the task that they gave me. In the afternoon they lashed me for not finishing the job, and the following day the same thing happened as on the previous day. Every day they lashed me unjustly because I did not finish what I did not know how to do, and thus I existed for many days until I found a way to escape; but I was tracked and they caught me like a fox; there they seized me by lasso as on the first occasion, and they carried me off to the mission, torturing me on the road. After we arrived, the father passed along the corridor of the house, and he ordered that they fasten me to the stake and **castigate**[6] me; they lashed me until I lost consciousness, and I did not regain consciousness for many hours afterwards. For several days I could not raise myself from the floor where they had laid me, and I still have on my shoulders the marks of the lashes which they gave me then.

---

[5] **recourse**—any way to turn for help.

[6] **castigate**—punish.

QUESTIONS TO CONSIDER

1. Why, do you think, did some Spanish and Mexican missionaries consider it acceptable to use any means—even violence—to convert Indians to Christianity?

2. What did the behavior of these priests indicate about their views of Native people?

3. How would you expect Janitin to feel about Christians after his capture and "conversion" by the mission priests?

Lecture to Missionary Cram

BY RED JACKET (SENECA)

Many Native Americans resisted attempts by whites to convert them to Christianity. Such a one was the principal chief of the Senecas, Sa-go-ye-wat-ha, who was better known as Red Jacket because of the British soldier's red coat he always wore. A gifted speaker, Red Jacket was born in 1752 and used his powers of persuasion to rise to become one of the most important leaders of the six nations of the Iroquois. He was an old man when a Protestant minister named Cram from the Boston Missionary Society told the Senecas in 1828, "There is but one religion, and but one way to serve God, and if you do not embrace the right way you cannot be happy together. You have never worshipped the Great Spirit in a manner acceptable to Him, but all your lives have been in great errors and darkness." Red Jacket listened patiently to Cram and then delivered the following reply.

Friend and Brother! . . . It was the will of the Great Spirit that we should meet together this day. He orders all things, and he has given us a fine day for our council.

He has taken his garment[1] from before the sun, and caused it to shine with brightness upon us. Our eyes are opened that we see clearly. Our ears are unstopped that we have been able to hear distinctly the words you have spoken. For all these favors we thank the Great Spirit, and him only.

Brother!—This council fire was **kindled**[2] by you. It was at your request that we came together at this time. We have listened with attention to what you have said. You requested us to speak our minds freely. This gives us great joy, for we now consider that we stand upright before you, and can speak what we think. All have heard your voice, and all speak to you as one man. Our minds are agreed.

Brother!—You say you want an answer to your talk before you leave this place. It is right you should have one, as you are a great distance from home, and we do not wish to **detain**[3] you. But we will first look back a little, and tell you what our fathers have told us, and what we have heard from the white people.

Brother!—Listen to what we say. There was a time when our forefathers owned this great island. Their **seats**[4] extended from the rising to the setting sun. The Great Spirit had made it for the use of Indians. He had created the buffalo, the deer, and other animals for food. He made the bear and the beaver, and their skins served us for clothing. He had scattered them over the country, and taught us how to take them. He had caused the earth to produce corn for bread. All this he had done for his red children because he loved them. If we had any disputes about hunting-grounds, they were generally settled without the shedding of much blood. But an evil day came upon us. Your forefathers crossed the great

---

[1] garment—clouds.

[2] **kindled**—built and set burning.

[3] **detain**—keep from proceeding; delay.

[4] **seats**—lands.

waters, and landed on this island. Their numbers were small. They found friends and not enemies. They told us they had fled their own country for fear of wicked men, and come here to enjoy their religion. They asked for a small seat. We took pity on them, granted their request, and they sat down amongst us. We gave them corn and meat. They gave us poison [alcohol] in return. The white people had now found our country. **Tidings**[5] were carried back, and more came amongst us. Yet we did not fear them. We took them to be friends. They called us brothers. We believed them, and gave them a larger seat. At length their numbers had greatly increased. They wanted more land. They wanted our country. Our eyes were opened, and our minds became uneasy. Wars took place. Indians were hired to fight against Indians, and many of our people were destroyed. They also brought strong liquors among us. It was strong and powerful, and has slain thousands.

Brother!—Our seats were once large, and yours were very small. You have now become a great people, and we have scarcely a place left to spread our blankets. You have got our country, but are not satisfied. You want to force your religion upon us.

Brother!—Continue to listen. You say that you are sent to instruct us how to worship the Great Spirit agreeably to his mind; and if we do not take hold of the religion which you white people teach, we shall be unhappy hereafter. You say that you are right and we are lost. How do we know this to be true? We understand that your religion is written in a book. If it was intended for us as well as for you, why has not the Great Spirit given it to us; and not only to us, but why did he not give to our forefathers the knowledge of that book, with the means of understanding it rightly? We only know what you tell us about

---

[5] **Tidings**—news reports.

it. How shall we know when to believe, being so often deceived by the white people?

Brother!—You say there is but one way to worship and serve the Great Spirit. If there is but one religion, why do you white people differ so much about it? Why not all agree, as you can all read the book?

Brother!—We do not understand these things. We are told that your religion was given to your forefathers, and has been handed down from father to son. We also have a religion which was given to our forefathers, and has been handed down to us their children. We worship that way. It teaches us to be thankful for all the favors we receive, to love each other, and to be united. We never quarrel about religion.

Brother!—The Great Spirit has made us all. But he has made a great difference between his white and red children. He has given us a different complexion and different customs. To you he has given the arts; to these he has not opened our eyes. We know these things to be true. Since he has made so great a difference between us in other things, why may we not conclude that he has given us a different religion, according to our understanding? The Great Spirit does right. He knows what is best for his children. We are satisfied.

Brother!—We do not wish to destroy your religion, or take it from you. We only want to enjoy our own.

Brother!—You say you have not come to get our land or our money, but to enlighten our minds. I will now tell you that I have been at your meetings and saw you collecting money from the meeting. I cannot tell what this money was intended for, but suppose it was for your minister; and if we should conform to your way of thinking, perhaps you may want some from us.

Brother!—We are told that you have been preaching to white people in this place. These people are our neighbors. We are acquainted with them. We will wait a little while, and see what effect your preaching has upon them. If we find it does them good and makes them honest and less **disposed**[6] to cheat Indians, we will then consider again what you have said.

Brother!—You have now heard our answer to your talk, and this is all we have to say at present. As we are going to part, we will come and take you by the hand, and hope the Great Spirit will protect you on your journey, and return you safe to your friends.

---

[6] **disposed**—willing.

QUESTIONS TO CONSIDER

1. What is your opinion of the missionary's statement that the Senecas had "never worshipped the Great Spirit in a manner acceptable to Him"?

2. How does Red Jacket believe Native people will be affected by the continued white expansion?

3. What arguments does Red Jacket use in defending different religious approaches by Indians and whites?

The Coming of the Black Robes

BY JULIA ANTELOPE NICODEMUS

(COEUR D'ALÊNE)

Because of their different colonial strategies, the British and French treated the Indians with whom they came in contact very differently. Generally, the French were interested mostly in trade, while the British wanted to expand their colonial settlements into Indian territories. While both the Catholic French and the Protestant British sought to convert the Indians to Christianity, the French Jesuit missionaries were usually more tolerant and accepting of Indian culture. In 1763, the French lost their territory in North America to the British, but the French Jesuits continued their missionary work. In 1841, the Jesuit priest Pierre de Smet and the Coeur d'Alêne people of Idaho encountered each other. The following story of this meeting was passed down orally for more than 100 years until 1954, when Julia Antelope Nicodemus, a Coeur d'Alêne woman, passed it on to a writer. Nicodemus had learned it from her mother-in-law, who was well acquainted with the oral history of her people.

Chief Whirling Black Crow was elected chief of the Coeur d'Alênes[1] because he was intelligent, and because he had initiative and other good qualities no other man in the tribe had.

One winter the snow was so deep that people could not hunt deer. They were on the brink of starvation. The chief had a song, a certain tune. It was his guardian spirit song. After he would sing a few minutes, deer would come running. So he told his people to be ready to shoot.

Chief Whirling Black Crow sang his song. The deer came running, and hunters shot them. People skinned the deer, quartered them, and piled up the pieces. Then everyone got a share. In those days people shared everything with the rest. After the chief sang his song, everybody had plenty of food.

One night the chief had a dream. A voice said to him, "Some day in the future you will have a teacher. You will know him because he will wear a black robe that comes to his ankles. He will wear a belt around his robe. Though his hair may be white, he will be like a boy in energy and strength."

Chief Whirling Black Crow thought that the teacher would come right away, but he didn't. Every time travelers came from a distance, the chief listened to their stories, always hoping to hear about the coming of the promised teacher. Many years passed, but he never forgot the dream and the promise. After he had grown old, he became ill with a lingering illness. One day he called to his bedside his son and his two daughters.

The son's name was *Silipstulew*, meaning "Earth-Going-Round-and-Round." To his son the dying chief said, "Keep on looking for the teacher. He will come, in

---

[1] Coeur d'Alênes—French name for a Native people of northern Idaho. The name means "heart of an owl" and was given to the tribe by the French traders who found them to be extremely clever and demanding when negotiating trade agreements.

time. When the Black Robe[2] comes, you do exactly as he tells you."

The old chief died, and Earth-Going-Round-and-Round became chief in his stead.

One day the new chief heard that there was a teacher down at Lapwai, among the Nez Percés.[3] He was teaching them something different from what they knew.

The chief said to his people living near Lake Coeur d'Alene, "Come with me, and we'll go to see this teacher. Perhaps he is the one my father said would come."

So they went to Lapwai, arriving late in the day. They exchanged food with the Nez Percés—camas for white camas, bitterroot for kouse[4]—as was the custom in those days. Next morning Chief Earth-Going-Round-and-Round said, "I want to see the new teacher."

The Nez Percés took him to the teacher and introduced him to the white man. Then the leader who had introduced them pointed to a house with a **veranda**.[5]

"There is where our teacher lives. Those are his children playing on the veranda."

Our chief was disappointed. The teacher did not wear a black robe. The teacher old Chief Whirling Black Crow had told him about did not have children. Chief Earth-Going-Round-and-Round knew that the dream had not come true yet.

"We will go home," he said to his people. "This is not the teacher my father told us about."

They waited a few more years.

---

[2] Black Robe—Catholic priest of the Society of Jesus, known as Jesuits. The Indians referred to the Jesuits as "black robes," because of the distinctive black cassocks they wore.

[3] Nez Percés—Indian people whose homeland lies just to the south of the Coeur d'Alênes' land.

[4] camas for white camas, bitterroot for kouse—Camas are the edible bulbs of a plant resembling the lily found in western North America. They are known for their sweetness. Bitterroot and kouse are edible fleshy plant roots that grow in the northwestern United States. The bitterroot plant produces pink flowers.

[5] veranda—covered or partially enclosed porch.

One year, at the time for catching white fish, many Coeur d'Alêne bands were camped along Lake Coeur d'Alene. They made a screen of twigs across the bay. The white fish would be stopped by the screen, and the men would dip up the fish in their nets. Then they would divide the fish among all the people in the villages.

One evening a man said to the chief, "Some Flatheads[6] are camping near here. There's a man with them that may be the teacher you're looking for. He's wearing a long black robe with a belt. And he has a book. He's walking back and forth near the camp."

The chief went to the other camp and shook hands with the Black Robe. Then he started to cry. "You are the man my father looked for, for many years, but did not see. A voice told him that you would come. Teach us what the voice said you would teach us."

The Black Robe was Father De Smet. He had with him a Cree who could speak Kalispel. The Coeur d'Alênes could understand Kalispel. Father De Smet taught the Coeur d'Alêne people for a few days. He taught them the Lord's Prayer, the Hail Mary, and the Apostles' Creed, in our language. He picked out some of the older boys and girls and taught each of them just a part of a prayer. And he told them that they should always stand in the same order when they repeated the prayer.

Then he said to them, "I must leave you now. If I do not come back, I will send somebody to teach you."

And he did. He sent two Black Robes from his mission among the Flatheads. They were Father Point and Father Huet. They started the mission among the Coeur d'Alênes.

---

[6] Flatheads—Indian tribe whose language is similar to that of the Coeur d'Alênes and who live just to the east of the Coeur d'Alênes and the Nez Percés near the border between Idaho and Montana.

QUESTIONS TO CONSIDER

1. What was life like for the Coeur d'Alênes when Chief Whirling Black Crow was their leader?

2. What did the Coeur d'Alênes believe that the Black Robes would do for them?

3. When they first met the Black Robe, how did the Coeur d'Alène people communicate with him?

4. Why do you think this story is important to the Coeur d'Alênes?

Wovoka, the Paiute Messiah

BY PORCUPINE (CHEYENNE)

By the late 1880s, the Indians of the Great Plains had lost their traditional homelands and were adjusting to a new and undesirable way of life on reservations. The populations of many tribes had seriously declined. At the same time, the United States Congress had passed a series of laws designed to remove the authority of tribal governments, break up tribal landholdings, and transform these Native Americans into independent farmers. In this situation, many Indians eagerly accepted the preaching and prophecy of a Paiute named Wovoka, whose father Tavibo had related visions of destruction and restoration of the old order to the Indians. Wovoka taught that because white men had killed the messiah, Christ, when he came to Earth the first time, God had returned Him to Earth again, this time in the person of an Indian, himself. Wovoka urged his followers to perform a ritual that became known as "the Ghost Dance," and the religion he established is known as the Ghost Dance Religion. The narrator of the following story, Porcupine, was a Cheyenne who traveled to see the messiah. A year later, in December 1890, troopers of the United States Seventh Cavalry brutally cut down members of this religion in the Massacre at Wounded Knee.

In November last [1889] I left the reservation with two other Cheyennes.[1] I went through [Fort] Washakie and took the Union Pacific railroad at Rawlins. We got on early in the morning about breakfast, rode all day on the railroad, and about dark reached a fort [possibly Bridger]. I stayed there two days, and then took a passenger train, and the next morning got to Fort Hall. I found some lodges of Snakes and Bannocks[2] there. I saw the agent[3] here, and he told me I could stay at the agency, but the chief of the Bannocks who was there took me to his camp near by. The Bannocks told me they were glad to see a Cheyenne and that we ought to make a treaty with the Bannocks.

The chief told me he had been to Washington and had seen the President, and that we ought all to be friends with the whites and live at peace with them and with each other. We talked these matters over for ten days. The agent then sent for me and some of the Bannocks and Shoshones, and asked me where I was going. I told him I was just traveling to meet other Indians and see other countries; that my people were at peace with the whites, and I thought I could travel any-where I wished. He asked me why I did not have a pass. I said because my agent would not give me one. He said he was glad to see me anyhow, and that the whites and Indians were all friends. Then he asked me where I wanted a pass to. I told him I wanted to go further and some Bannocks and Shoshones wanted to go along. He gave passes—five of them—to the chiefs of the three

---

[1] By the time of this writing, the Cheyenne had been forced from their original homelands on the northern Great Plains onto reservations in northern and western Oklahoma.

[2] lodges of Snakes and Bannocks—log and earthen homes occupied by Snake and Bannock people. The name "Snake" is sometimes used by groups of Paiute, Shoshone, and Bannock Indians who originally lived in the mountain and basin regions of the western United States. The Bannocks were a tribe originally from southern Idaho.

[3] agent—representative of the United States Bureau of Indian Affairs who supervised the reservation.

parties. We took the railroad to a little town near by, and then took a narrow-gauge road.[4] We went on this, riding all night at a very fast rate of speed, and came to a town on a big lake [Ogden or Salt Lake City]. We stayed there one day, taking the cars[5] at night, rode all night, and the next morning about 9 o'clock saw a settlement of Indians. We traveled south, going on a narrow-gauge road. We got off at this Indian town. The Indians here were different from any Indians I ever saw. The women and men were dressed in white people's clothes, the women having their hair banged.[6] These Indians had their faces painted white with black spots. We stayed with these people all day. We took the same road at night and kept on. We traveled all night, and about daylight we saw a lot of houses, and they told us there were a lot more Indians there; so we got off, and there is where we saw Indians living in huts of grass. We stopped here and got something to eat. There were whites living near by. We got on the cars again at night, and during the night we got off among some Indians, who were fish-eaters [Paiute]. We stayed among the fish-eaters till morning, and then got into a wagon with the son of the chief of the fish-eaters, and we arrived about noon at an agency on a big river. There was also a big lake near the agency.

The agent asked us where we were from and said we were a long ways from home, and that he would write to our agent and let him know we were all right. From this agency we went back to the station, and they told us there were some more Indians to the south. One of the chiefs of the fish-eaters then furnished us with four wagons. We traveled all day, and then came to another

---

[4] narrow-gauge road—small railroad line on which the width of the track is narrower than that of a "standard-gauge" railroad.

[5] cars—railroad cars for passengers. Before the invention of the automobile, the term *cars* was commonly used in America to mean train cars.

[6] hair banged—cut in "bangs" across their forehead. At the time only white women usually wore their hair in this fashion.

railroad. We left our wagons here and took the railroad, the fish-eaters telling us there were some more Indians along the railroad who wanted to see us. We took this railroad about 2 o'clock and about sundown got to another agency, where there were more fish-eaters. [From diagrams drawn and explanations given of them in addition to the foregoing, there seems to be no doubt that the lakes visited are Pyramid and Walker lakes in western Nevada, and the agencies those of the same name.]

They told us they had heard from the Shoshone agency[7] that the people in this country were all bad people, but that they were good people there. All the Indians from the Bannock agency down to where I finally stopped danced this dance [referring to the late religious dances at the Cheyenne agency], the whites often dancing it themselves. [It will be recollected that he traveled constantly through the Mormon country.][8] I knew nothing about this dance before going. I happened to run across it, that is all. I will tell you about it. [Here all the Indian **auditors**[9] removed their hats in token that the talk to follow was to be on a religious subject.] I want you all to listen to this, so that there will be no mistake. There is no harm in what I am to say to anyone. I heard this where I met my friends in Nevada. It is a wonder you people never heard this before. In the dance we had there [Nevada] the whites and Indians danced together. I met there a great many kinds of people, but all seemed to know all about this religion. The people there seemed all to be good. I never saw any drinking or fighting or bad conduct among them. They treated me well on the cars, without pay. They gave me food without charge, and I found that this was a habit among them toward

---

[7] Shoshone agency—the office of the Bureau of Indian Affairs that supervised the Shoshone reservations.

[8] Mormon country—the state of Utah, home of the Mormons, the name given to members of the Church of Jesus Christ of Latter Day Saints.

[9] **auditors**—listeners.

their neighbors. I thought it strange that the people there should have been so good, so different from those here.

What I am going to say is the truth. The two men sitting near me were with me, and will bear witness that I speak the truth. I and my people have been living in ignorance until I went and found out the truth. All the whites and Indians are brothers, I was told there. I never knew this before.

The fish-eaters near Pyramid lake told me that Christ had appeared on earth again.[10] They said Christ knew he was coming; that eleven of his children were also coming from a far land. It appeared that Christ had sent for me to go there, and that was why unconsciously I took my journey. It had been **foreordained**.[11] Christ had summoned myself and others from all heathen tribes, from two to three or four from each of fifteen or sixteen different tribes. There were more different languages than I ever heard before and I did not understand any of them. They told me when I got there that my great father was there also, but did not know who he was. The people assembled called a council, and the chief's son went to see the Great Father [messiah], who sent word to us to remain fourteen days in that camp and that he would come to see us. He sent me a small package of something white to eat that I did not know the name of. There were a great many people in the council, and this white food was divided among them. The food was a big white nut. Then I went to the agency at Walker lake and they told us Christ would be there in two days. At the end of two days, on the third morning, hundreds of people gathered at this place. They cleared off a place near the agency in the form of a circus ring and we all gathered there. This space was perfectly cleared of grass, etc. We waited there till late in the evening anxious to see

---

[10] Christ had appeared on earth again—a reference to the belief that Wovoka, the Paiute Indian, was the messiah who would save the Indian people.

[11] **foreordained**—determined at an earlier time as in a prophecy.

Christ. Just before sundown I saw a great many people, mostly Indians, coming dressed in white men's clothes. The Christ was with them. They all formed in this ring around it [the cleared space]. They put up sheets all around the circle, as they had no tents. Just after dark some of the Indians told me that the Christ [Father] was arrived. I looked around to find him, and finally saw him sitting on one side of the ring. They all started toward him to see him. They made a big fire to throw light on him. I never looked around, but went forward, and when I saw him I bent my head. I had always thought the Great Father was a white man, but this man looked like an Indian. He sat there a long time and nobody went up to speak to him. He sat with his head bowed all the time. After awhile he rose and said he was very glad to see his children. "I have sent for you and am glad to see you. I am going to talk to you awhile about your relatives who are dead and gone. My children, I want you to listen to all I have to say to you. I will teach you, too, how to dance a dance, and I want you to dance it. Get ready for your dance and then, when the dance is over, I will talk to you." He was dressed in a white coat with stripes. The rest of his dress was a white man's except that he had on a pair of moccasins. Then he commenced our dance, everybody joining in, the Christ singing while we danced. We danced till late in the night, when he told us we had danced enough.

The next morning, after breakfast was over, we went into the circle and spread canvas over it on the ground, the Christ standing in the midst of us. He told us he was going away that day, but would be back that next morning and talk to us.

In the night when I first saw him I thought he was an Indian, but the next day when I could see better he looked different. He was not so dark as an Indian, not so light as a white man. He had no beard or whiskers, but very heavy eyebrows. He was a good-looking man. We were crowded up very close. We had been told that nobody was to talk, and even if we whispered the Christ would know it. I had heard that Christ had been crucified, and I looked to see, and I saw a scar on his wrist and one on his face, and he seemed to be the man. I could not see his feet. He would talk to us all day.

That evening we all assembled again to see him depart. When we were assembled, he began to sing, and he commenced to tremble all over, violently for a while, and then sat down. We danced all that night, the Christ lying down beside us apparently dead.

The next morning when we went to eat breakfast, the Christ was with us. After breakfast four **heralds**[12] went around and called out that the Christ was back with us and wanted to talk with us. The circle was prepared again. The people assembled, and Christ came among us and sat down. He said he wanted to talk to us again and for us to listen. He said: "I am the man who made everything you see around you. I am not lying to you, my children. I made this earth and everything on it. I have been to heaven and seen your dead friends and have seen my own father and mother. In the beginning, after God made the earth, they sent me back to teach the people, and when I came back on earth the people were afraid of me and treated me badly. This is what they did to me [showing his scars]. I did not try to defend myself. I found my children were bad, so went back to heaven and left them. My father told me the earth was getting old and worn out, and the people getting bad, and that I was to renew everything as it used to be, and make it better."

He told us also that all our dead were to be resurrected; that they were all to come back to earth, and that as the earth was too small for them and us, he would do away with heaven, and make the earth itself large enough to contain us all; that we must tell all the people

---

[12] **heralds**—messengers.

we meet about these things. He spoke to us about fighting, and said that was bad, and we must keep from it; that the earth was to be all good hereafter, and we must all be friends with one another. He said that in the fall of the year the youth of all the good people would be renewed, so that nobody would be more than 40 years old, and that if they behaved themselves well after this the youth of everyone would be renewed in the spring. He said if we were all good he would send people among us who could heal all our wounds and sickness by mere touch, and that we would live forever. He told us not to quarrel, or fight, nor strike each other, nor shoot one another; that the whites and Indians were to be all one people. He said if any man disobeyed what he ordered, his tribe would be wiped from the face of the earth; that we must believe everything he said, and that we must not doubt him, or say he lied; that if we did, he would know it; that he would know our thoughts and actions, in no matter what part of the world we might be.

When I heard this from the Christ, and came back home to tell it to my people, I thought they would listen. Where I went to there were lots of white people, but I never had one of them say an unkind word to me. I thought all of your people knew all of this I have told you of, but it seems you do not.

Ever since the Christ I speak of talked to me I have thought what he said was good. I see nothing bad in it. When I got back, I knew my people were bad, and had heard nothing of all this, so I got them together and told them of it and warned them to listen to it for their own good. I talked to them for four nights and five days. I told them just what I have told you here today. I told them what I said were the words of God Almighty, who was looking down on them. I wish some of you had been up in our camp here to have heard my words to the Cheyennes. The only bad thing that there has been in it at all was this: I had just told my people that the Christ would visit the sins of any Indian upon the whole tribe, when the recent trouble [killing of Ferguson] occurred. If any one of you think I am not telling the truth, you can go and see this man I speak of for yourselves. I will go with you, and I would like one or two of my people who doubt me to go with me.

The Christ talked to us all in our respective tongues. You can see this man in your sleep any time you want after you have seen him and shaken hands with him once. Through him you can go to heaven and meet your friends. Since my return I have seen him often in my sleep. About the time the soldiers went up to Rosebud[13] I was lying in my lodge asleep, when this man appeared and told me that the Indians had gotten into trouble, and I was frightened. The next night he appeared to me and told me that everything would come out all right.

---

[13] Rosebud—a Sioux reservation in South Dakota. In 1890, U.S. troops were sent there to stop the practice of the Ghost Dance Religion.

QUESTIONS TO CONSIDER

1. What evidence does Porcupine, the narrator, give to explain that his travels were unusual?

2. What observations does Porcupine make about the appearance of the Indians he meets on his travels?

3. What struck Porcupine as unusual about the appearance of the man he called "the Christ"?

4. What were the problems of the Indian people that Wovoka, called the Christ, felt that he could solve?

5. What support can you find in this narrative that Porcupine believed in the teachings of Wovoka?

Religion

▲

Mandan Indians perform the Bison Dance in front of their medicine lodge. The Bison Dance was performed to ensure future success in the hunt.

◀ A Native American doctor makes medicine in his home. In many Native cultures, medicine was linked with religion and was created from native plants by a shaman or other religious figure.

A mural shows ceremonial figures in Kuaua Pueblo, New Mexico.
▼

The Hopi Snake Dance is performed annually for nine days in August. The dance is an expression of the desire for rain. The Hopi believe that rattlesnakes and other snakes can influence rain.

▼

Resistance

chapter three

Eyewitness to the Pueblo Uprising

BY PEDRO NARANJO (PUEBLO)
AS RECORDED IN SPANISH RECORDS

By the late 1500s, the Spanish had moved northward from Mexico into what is now New Mexico and Arizona and had conquered the Pueblo people, a culture made up of many tribes and languages. The Spaniards' first contact with the Pueblos involved an effort to convert them to Christianity. However, the Spanish regarded the Pueblos as inferiors and often treated them cruelly, demanding that they pay high taxes in the form of labor, crops, and goods. The Pueblos planned a revolt in 1680, despite knowing they would be severely punished if they failed to succeed. After an earlier rebellion, the Spanish had retaliated by killing hundreds of Indians. Thus, Popé, the leader of the 1680 uprising, made his plans with the utmost secrecy, and the Pueblos succeeded in driving out the Spanish for twelve years. In 1681, Pedro Naranjo, a Pueblo man, gave the following account of the uprising to Spanish government officials, who added their own comments.

In the said *plaza de armas*[1] on the said day, month, and year, for the prosecution of the judicial proceedings of this case his lordship caused to appear before him an Indian prisoner named Pedro Naranjo, a native of the pueblo of San Felipe, of the Queres nation,[2] who was captured in the advance and attack upon the pueblo of La Isleta. He makes himself understood very well in the Castilian language and speaks his mother tongue and the Tegua.[3] He took the oath in due legal form in the name of God, our Lord, and a sign of the cross, under charge of which he promised to tell the truth concerning what he knows and as he might be questioned, and having understood the seriousness of the oath and so signified through the interpreters, he spoke as indicated by the contents of the *autos*.[4]

Asked whether he knows the reason or motives which the Indians of this kingdom had for rebelling, forsaking the law of God and obedience to his Majesty, and committing such grave and atrocious crimes, and who were the leaders and principal movers, and by whom and how it was ordered; and why they burned the images, temples, crosses, rosaries, and things of divine worship, committing such atrocities as killing priests, Spaniards, women, and children, and the rest that he might know touching the question, he said that since the government of Señor General Hernando

---

[1] *plaza de armas*—Spanish term meaning the "place of arms, or weapons"; the center of a Spanish colonial town where the military and government buildings are located.

[2] pueblo of San Felipe, of the Queres nation—*Pueblo* is a Spanish term for an Indian village, particularly those of the Pueblo people of northwestern New Mexico and northeastern Arizona during the period of Spanish colonial rule. This particular village was named for St. Philip. The Queres (or Keres) people were part of the Pueblo culture living along the upper Rio Grande.

[3] Castilian language . . . his mother tongue and the Tegua—Castilian is the Spanish dialect spoken by the European authorities. The mother tongue refers to the Queres (Keres) language spoken by the prisoner, Pedro Naranjo. The Tegua (or Tewa) language is one of several different languages spoken by the various groups of the Pueblo people.

[4] *autos*—Spanish term meaning "acts" or official government documents or papers such as the recorded testimony of Pedro Naranjo.

Ugarte y la Concha[5] they had planned to rebel on various occasions through conspiracies of the Indian sorcerers, and that although in some pueblos the messages were accepted, in other parts they would not agree to it; and that it is true that during the government of the said señor general seven or eight Indians were hanged for this same cause, whereupon the unrest subsided. Some time thereafter they [the conspirators] sent from the pueblo of Los Taos through the pueblos of the custodia[6] two deerskins with some pictures on them signifying conspiracy after their manner, in order to **convoke**[7] the people to a new rebellion, and the said deerskins passed to the province of Moqui, where they refused to accept them. The pact which they had been forming ceased for the time being, but they always kept in their hearts the desire to carry it out, so as to live as they are living today. Finally, in the past years, at the summons of an Indian named Popé[8] who is said to have communication with the devil, it happened that in an *estufa*[9] of the pueblo of Los Taos there appeared to the said Popé three figures of Indians who never came out of the estufa. They gave the said Popé to understand that they were going underground to the lake of Copala.[10] He saw these figures emit fire from all the extremities of their bodies, and that one of them was called Caudi, another Tilini, and the other Tleume; and these three beings spoke to the said Popé, who was in hiding from the secretary, Francisco Xavier,

---

[5] Señor General Hernando Ugarte y la Concha—the Spanish governor of New Mexico in the 1650s.

[6] pueblos of the custodia—the villages in which there were Spanish soldiers or guards.

[7] **convoke**—provoke.

[8] Popé (or Po' pay)—a Tewa Indian from the pueblo of San Juan on the Rio Grande. He was the leader of the Pueblo Rebellion against the Spanish.

[9] *estufa*—an underground room (also called a kiva) used for Pueblo Indian religious ceremonies. It often contained fire pits, altars, and an opening in the floor believed to connect to the realm of the spirit world.

[10] lake of Copala—the spiritual homeland of the Pueblo. They believed that they had originally arrived on Earth from this place.

who wished to punish him as a sorcerer. They told him to make a cord of **maguey**[11] fiber and tie some knots in it which would signify the number of days that they must wait before the rebellion. He said that the cord was passed through all the pueblos of the kingdom so that the ones which agreed to it [the rebellion] might untie one knot in sign of obedience, and by the other knots they would know the days which were lacking; and this was to be done on pain of death to those who refused to agree to it. As a sign of agreement and notice of having concurred in the treason and **perfidy**[12] they were to send up smoke signals to that effect in each one of the pueblos singly. The said cord was taken from pueblo to pueblo by the swiftest youths under the penalty of death if they revealed the secret. Everything being thus arranged, two days before the time set for its execution, because his lordship had learned of it and had imprisoned two Indian accomplices from the pueblo of Tesuque, it was carried out prematurely that night, because it seemed to them that they were now discovered; and they killed **religious**,[13] Spaniards, women, and children. This being done, it was proclaimed in all the pueblos that everyone in common should obey the commands of their father whom they did not know, which would be given through El Caydi or El Popé. This was heard by Alonso Catiti, who came to the pueblo of this **declarant**[14] to say that everyone must unite to go to the villa to kill the governor and the Spaniards who had remained with him, and that he who did not obey would, on their return, be beheaded; and in fear of this they agreed to it. Finally the señor governor and those who were with him escaped from the siege, and later this declarant saw that

---

[11] **maguey**—plant used to make rope.

[12] **perfidy**—treachery.

[13] **religious**—Catholic priests or other members of the clergy.

[14] **declarant**—one who declares or testifies, in this case the Indian Pedro Naranjo.

as soon as the Spaniards had left the kingdom an order came from the said Indian, Popé, in which he commanded all the Indians to break the lands and enlarge their cultivated fields, saying that now they were as they had been in ancient times, free from the labor they had performed for the religious and the Spaniards, who could not now be alive. He said that this is the legitimate cause and the reason they had for rebelling, because they had always desired to live as they had when they came out of the lake of Copala. Thus he replies to the question.

Asked for what reason they so blindly burned the images, temples, crosses, and other things of divine worship, he stated that the said Indian, Popé, came down in person, and with him El Saca and El Chato from the pueblo of Los Taos, and other captains and leaders and many people who were in his train, and he ordered in all the pueblos through which he passed that they instantly break up and burn the images of the holy Christ, the Virgin Mary and the other saints, the crosses, and everything pertaining to Christianity, and that they burn the temples, break up the bells, and separate from the wives whom God had given them in marriage[15] and take those whom they desired. In order to take away their baptismal names, the water, and the holy oils, they were to plunge into the rivers and wash themselves with amole, which is a root native to the country, washing even their clothing, with the understanding that there would thus be taken from them the character of the holy sacraments. They did this, and also many other things which he does not recall, given to understand that this mandate had come from the Caydi and the other two who emitted fire from their extremities in the said estufa of Taos, and that they thereby returned to the state of

---

[15] The Spanish Catholic priests had placed many of the Indians in forced marriages with other Indians who had been converted to Christianity.

their **antiquity**,[16] as when they came from the lake of Copala; that this was the better life and the one they desired, because the God of the Spaniards was worth nothing and theirs was very strong, the Spaniard's God being rotten wood. These things were observed and obeyed by all except some who, moved by the zeal of Christians, opposed it, and such persons the said Popé caused to be killed immediately. He saw to it that they at once erected and rebuilt their houses of idolatry which they call estufas, and made very ugly masks in imitation of the devil in order to dance the dance of the cacina;[17] and he said likewise that the devil had given them to understand that living thus in accordance with the law of their ancestors, they would harvest a great deal of maize, many beans, a great abundance of cotton, calabashes,[18] and very large watermelons and cantaloupes; and that they could erect their houses and enjoy abundant health and leisure. As he has said, the people were very much pleased, living at their ease in this life of their antiquity, which was the chief cause of their falling into such laxity. Following what has already been stated, in order to terrorize them further and cause them to observe the **diabolical**[19] commands, there came to them a pronouncement from the three demons already described, and from El Popé, to the effect that he who might still keep in his heart a regard for the priests, the governor, and the Spaniards would be known from his unclean face and clothes, and would be punished. And he stated that the said four persons stopped at nothing to have their commands obeyed. Thus he replies to the question.

---

[16] **antiquity**—ancient past.

[17] the dance of the cacina—ceremonial dance to summon spirits.

[18] calabashes—gourds.

[19] **diabolical**—relating to or coming from a devil or fiend.

Asked what arrangements and plans they had made for the **contingency**[20] of the Spaniards' return, he said that what he knows concerning the question is that they were always saying they would have to fight to the death, for they do not wish to live in any other way than they are living at present; and the demons in the estufa of Taos had given them to understand that as soon as the Spaniards began to move toward this kingdom they would warn them so that they might unite, and none of them would be caught. He having been questioned further and repeatedly touching the case, he said that he has nothing more to say except that they should be always on the alert, because the said Indians were continually planning to follow the Spaniards and fight with them by night, in order to drive off the horses and catch them afoot, although they might have to follow them for many leagues.[21] What he has said is the truth, and what happened, on the word of a Christian who confesses his guilt. He said that he has come to the pueblos through fear to lead in **idolatrous**[22] dances, in which he greatly fears in his heart that he may have offended God, and that now having been absolved and returned to the fold of the church, he has spoken the truth in everything he has been asked.

---

[20] **contingency**—possibility.

[21] for many leagues—a long way. *League* is a general term for a unit of distance, usually much longer than a mile, that varies depending on the country in which it is used.

[22] **idolatrous**—relating to the worship of idols or false gods.

QUESTIONS TO CONSIDER

1. How did the Pueblo people spread news of the planned revolt?

2. What were the differences between the traditional religion of the Pueblo people and that of the Spanish Christians?

3. How can you tell whether the writer of this testimony was a believer in the Christian religion or in the traditional Pueblo religion?

4. How did Popé and his followers plan to remove the influence of the Christian faith from their villages?

5. What did the Pueblos believe would happen once they returned to practicing the traditional religion of their ancestors?

Plea to the Choctaws and the Chickasaws

BY TECUMSEH (SHAWNEE)

By the early 1800s, white settlers were pushing westward into the North American interior more rapidly and in larger numbers than ever before. Many Native American leaders realized that unified resistance by an alliance of Indian tribes was the only way to hold on to their lands and way of life. Tecumseh, the great chief of the Shawnee people, was the strongest advocate of this strategy. In 1811, Tecumseh spent six months speaking to Indian tribes throughout the southeastern United States. The homeland of the Choctaws and Chickasaws in what is now Tennessee and Mississippi was seriously threatened, and it was to these tribes that Tecumseh delivered the following call to action. The Chickasaws rejected his plea. In the War of 1812, Tecumseh supported the British and led a force of Indians against the Americans at Detroit. The following year in Indiana, Tecumseh was killed in battle, and his plans for an independent Indian nation died with him.

In view of questions of vast importance, have we met together in solemn council tonight. Nor should we here debate whether we have been wronged and injured, but by what measures we should avenge ourselves; for our merciless oppressors, having long since planned out their proceedings, are not about to make, but have and are still making attacks upon our race who have as yet come to no **resolution**.[1] Nor are we ignorant by steps, and by what gradual advances, the whites break in upon our neighbors. Imagining themselves to be still undiscovered, they show themselves the less **audacious**[2] because you are **insensible**.[3] The whites are already nearly a match for us all united, and too strong for any one tribe alone to resist; so that unless we support one another with our collective and united forces; unless every tribe unanimously combines to give check to the ambition and **avarice**[4] of the whites, they will soon conquer us apart and disunited, and we will be driven away from our native country and scattered as autumnal leaves before the wind.

But have we not enough courage remaining to defend our country and maintain our ancient independence? Will we calmly suffer the white intruders and tyrants to enslave us? Shall it be said of our race that we knew not how to **extricate**[5] ourselves from the three most dreadful calamities—folly, inactivity, and cowardice? But what need is there to speak of the past? It speaks for itself and asks, Where today is the Pequod? Where the Narragansetts, the Mohawks, Pocanokets, and many other once powerful tribes of our race?[6] They

---

[1] **resolution**—final decision.

[2] **audacious**—bold.

[3] **insensible**—unaware.

[4] **avarice**—greed.

[5] **extricate**—remove; escape.

[6] Pequod, Narragansetts, Mohawks, Pocanokets—northeastern Native American people who were conquered by European whites.

have vanished before the avarice and oppression of the white men, as snow before a summer sun. In the vain hope of alone defending their ancient possessions, they have fallen in the wars with the white men. Look abroad over their once beautiful country, and what see you now? **Naught**[7] but the ravages of the pale face destroyers[8] meet our eyes. So it will be with you Choctaws and Chickasaws! Soon your mighty forest trees, under the shade of whose wide spreading branches you have played in infancy, sported in boyhood, and now rest your wearied limbs after the fatigue of the chase, will be cut down to fence in the land which the white intruders dare to call their own. Soon their broad roads will pass over the grave of your fathers, and the place of their rest will be blotted out forever. The **annihilation**[9] of our race is at hand unless we unite in one common cause against the common foe. Think not, brave Choctaws and Chickasaws, that you can remain passive and indifferent to the common danger, and thus escape the common fate. Your people, too, will soon be as falling leaves and scattering clouds before their **blighting**[10] breath. You, too, will be driven away from your native land and ancient domains as leaves are driven before the wintry storms.

Sleep not longer, O Choctaws and Chickasaws, in false security and **delusive**[11] hopes. Our broad domains are fast escaping from our grasp. Every year our white intruders become more greedy, exacting, oppressive, and overbearing. Every year **contentions**[12] spring up between them and our people and when blood is shed we have to make atonement whether right or wrong, at the cost of the lives of our greatest chiefs, and the yielding

---

[7] **Naught**—nothing.

[8] pale face destroyers—white people.

[9] **annihilation**—total destruction.

[10] **blighting**—killing or destroying.

[11] **delusive**—false.

[12] **contentions**—acts of rivalry; quarrels.

up of large tracts of our lands. Before the pale faces came among us, we enjoyed the happiness of unbounded freedom, and were acquainted with neither riches, wants nor oppression. How is it now? Wants and oppression are our lot; for are we not controlled in everything, and dare we move without asking, by your leave? Are we not being stripped day by day of the little that remains of our ancient liberty? Do they not even kick and strike us as they do their black-faces?[13] How long will it be before they will tie us to a post and whip us, and make us work for them in their cornfields as they do them? Shall we wait for that moment or shall we die fighting before submitting to such **ignominy**?[14]

Have we not for years had before our eyes a sample of their designs, and are they not sufficient **harbingers**[15] of their future determinations? Will we not soon be driven from our respective countries and the graves of our ancestors? Will not the bones of our dead be plowed up, and their graves be turned into fields? Shall we calmly wait until they become so numerous that we will no longer be able to resist oppression? Will we wait to be destroyed in our turn, without making an effort worthy of our race? Shall we give up our homes, our country, **bequeathed**[16] to us by the Great Spirit, the graves of our dead, and everything that is dear and sacred to us, without a struggle? I know you will cry with me: Never! Never! Then let us by unity of action destroy them all, which we now can do, or drive them back whence they came. War or extermination is now our only choice. Which do you choose? I know your answer. Therefore, I now call on you, brave Choctaws and Chickasaws, to assist in the just cause of liberating our race from the grasp of our faithless invaders and heartless oppressors.

---

[13] black-faces—African slaves.

[14] **ignominy**—humiliation or dishonor.

[15] **harbingers**—indications of what will occur in the future.

[16] **bequeathed**—given as an inheritance.

The white **usurpation**[17] in our common country must be stopped, or we, its rightful owners, be forever destroyed and wiped out as a race of people. I am now at the head of many warriors backed by the strong arm of English soldiers. Choctaws and Chickasaws, you have too long borne with grievous usurpation inflicted by the arrogant Americans. Be no longer their **dupes**.[18] If there be one here tonight who believes that his rights will not sooner or later be taken from him by the avaricious American pale faces, his ignorance ought to excite pity, for he knows little of the character of our common foe.

And if there be one among you mad enough to undervalue the growing power of the white race among us, let him tremble in considering the fearful woes he will bring down upon our entire race, if by his criminal indifference he assists the designs of our common enemy against our common country. Then listen to the voice of duty, of honor, of nature and of your endangered country. Let us form one body, one heart, and defend to the last warrior our country, our homes, our liberty, and the graves of our fathers.

Choctaws and Chickasaws, you are among the few of our race who sit **indolently**[19] at ease. You have indeed enjoyed the reputation of being brave, but will you be indebted for it more from report than fact? Will you let the whites **encroach**[20] upon your domains even to your very door before you will assert your rights in resistance? Let no one in this council imagine that I speak more from malice against the pale face Americans than just grounds of complaint. Complaint is just toward friends who have failed in their duty; accusation is against enemies guilty of injustice. And surely, if any

---

[17] **usurpation**—seizure by force.

[18] **dupes**—easily deceived people, used as the tool of others.

[19] **indolently**—lazily.

[20] **encroach**—advance against; take another's possessions or rights gradually or stealthily.

people ever had, we have good and just reasons to believe we have **ample**[21] grounds to accuse the Americans of injustice; especially when such great acts of injustice have been committed by them upon our race, of which they seem to have no manner of regard, or even to reflect. They are a people fond of innovations, quick to contrive and quick to put their schemes into effectual execution no matter how great the wrong and injury to us; while we are content to preserve what we already have. Their designs are to enlarge their possessions by taking yours in turn; and will you, can you longer **dally**,[22] O Choctaws and Chickasaws?

Do you imagine that that people will not continue longest in the enjoyment of peace who timely prepare to **vindicate**[23] themselves, and manifest a determined resolution to do themselves right whenever they are wronged? Far otherwise. Then haste to the belief of our common cause, as by **consanguinity**[24] of blood you are bound; lest the day be not far distant when you will be left single-handed and alone to the cruel mercy of our most **inveterate**[25] foe.

---

[21] **ample**—great enough; fully sufficient.

[22] **dally**—waste time; dawdle.

[23] **vindicate**—justify; prove themselves worthy.

[24] **consanguinity**—related by a common ancestor.

[25] **inveterate**—long-established.

QUESTIONS TO CONSIDER

1. Why did Tecumseh criticize the Choctaws and Chickasaws?

2. Why did Tecumseh feel that it was important for the Choctaws and Chickasaws to join forces with him?

3. How, according to Tecumseh, had life changed for the Indian people since the arrival of the whites? How would it continue to change?

The Great Sioux Uprising

BY BIG EAGLE (SANTEE SIOUX)

In American popular culture, the most familiar image of Native
Americans in the 1800s is largely based on the Sioux people of the
Great Plains. There were many groups within the Sioux nation, such
as the Oglala, Lakota, and Santee. They dwelt in tipis, traveled on
horseback, and hunted buffalo, on which they depended for food,
clothing, and shelter. Beginning in the mid-1850s, the Sioux resisted
the influx of white settlers. Armed conflict with the United States
continued for nearly half a century with the Sioux people being
driven continually westward. The following is an account of the 1862
Santee Sioux Uprising in Minnesota, which occurred while the United
States was engaged in the Civil War. The narrator, Big Eagle, was a
Santee Sioux who took part in the fighting. Big Eagle's story helps
explain the many reasons why his people chose to resist and the
complicated situation in which they found themselves. After the
uprising was put down, more than 2,000 Santee Sioux, including Big
Eagle, were imprisoned by the United States government.

Of the causes that led to the outbreak of August, 1862, much has been said. Of course it was wrong, as we all know now, but there were not many Christians among the Indians then, and they did not understand things as they should. There was great dissatisfaction among the Indians over many things the whites did. The whites would not let them go to war against their enemies. This was right, but the Indians did not then know it. Then the whites were always trying to make the Indians give up their life and live like white men—go to farming, work hard and do as they did—and the Indians did not know how to do that, and did not want to anyway. It seemed too sudden to make such a change. If the Indians had tried to make the whites live like them, the whites would have resisted, and it was the same way with many Indians. The Indians wanted to live as they did before the treaty of Traverse des Sioux[1]—go where they pleased and when they pleased; hunt game wherever they could find it, sell their furs to the traders, and live as they could.

Then the Indians did not think the traders had done right. The Indians bought goods [from] them on credit, and when the government payments came the traders were on hand with their books, which showed that the Indians owed so much and so much, and as the Indians kept no books they could not deny their accounts, but had to pay them, and sometimes the traders got all their money. I do not say that the traders always cheated and lied about these accounts. I know many of them were honest men and kind and accommodating, but since I have been a citizen I know that many white men, when they go to pay their accounts, often think them too large and refuse to pay them, and they go to law about them and there is much bad feeling. The Indians could not go to law, but there was always trouble over their credits.

---

[1] In 1851, the Sioux people sold all of their land in western and southern Minnesota to the United States government.

Under the treaty of Traverse des Sioux the Indians had to pay a very large sum of money to the traders for old debts, some of which ran back fifteen years, and many of those who had got the goods were dead and others were not present, and the traders' books had to be received as to the amounts, and the money was taken from the tribe to pay them. Of course the traders often were of great service to the Indians in letting them have goods on credit, but the Indians seemed to think the traders ought not to be too hard on them about the payments, but do as the Indians did among one another, and put off the payment until they were better able to make it.

Then many of the white men often abused the Indians and treated them unkindly. Perhaps they had excuses, but the Indians did not think so. Many of the whites always seemed to say by their manner when they saw an Indian, "I am much better than you," and the Indians did not like this. There was [an] excuse for this, but the Dakotas[2] did not believe there were better men in the world than they. Then some of the white men abused the Indian women in a certain way and disgraced them, and surely there was no excuse for that.

All these things made many Indians dislike the whites. Then a little while before the outbreak there was trouble among the Indians themselves. Some of the Indians took a sensible course and began to live like white men. The government built them houses, furnished them tools, seed, etc., and taught them to farm. At the two agencies,[3] Yellow Medicine and Redwood, there were several hundred acres of land in cultivation that summer. Others stayed in their teepees.

---

[2] Dakotas—Native American people better known as the Sioux.

[3] agencies—the headquarters or offices of the U.S. Bureau of Indian Affairs, which administered Indian reservations and attempted to turn the nomadic Plains Indians into farmers.

There was a white man's party and an Indian party.[4] We had politics among us and there was much feeling.

A new chief speaker for the tribe was to be elected. There were three candidates—Little Crow,[5] myself, and Wa-sui-hi-ya-ye-dan ("Traveling Hail"). After an exciting contest Traveling Hail was elected. Little Crow felt sore over his defeat. Many of our tribe believed him responsible for the sale of the north ten-mile strip, and I think this was why he was defeated. I did not care much about it. Many whites think that Little Crow was the principal chief of the Dakotas at this time, but he was not. Wabasha was the principal chief, and he was of the white man's party; so was I; so was old Shakopee, whose band was very large. Many think if old Shakopee had lived there would have been no war, for he was for the white men and had great influence. But he died that summer, and was succeeded by his son [called Shakopee]. . . . This Shakopee was against the white men. He took part in the outbreak, murdering women and children, but I never saw him in a battle, and he was caught in Manitoba[6] and hanged in 1864. My brother, Medicine Bottle, was hanged with him.

As the summer advanced, there was great trouble among the Sioux—troubles among themselves, troubles with the whites, and one thing and another. The war with the South[7] was going on then, and a great many men had left the state and gone down there to fight. A few weeks before the outbreak the President[8] called for many more men, and a great many of the white men of

---

[4] white man's party and an Indian party—a group of Sioux people who favored cooperation with the United States government and the adopting of white ways and a second group who favored retaining traditional Indian ways of life.

[5] Little Crow—leader of the Santee Sioux uprising of 1862.

[6] Manitoba—a province in south central Canada.

[7] war with the South—American Civil War (1861–65).

[8] the President—Abraham Lincoln, president of the United States (1861–65).

Minnesota and some half-breeds[9] enlisted and went to Fort Snelling[10] to be sent [to the war in the] South. We understood that the South was getting the best of the fight, and it was said that the North would be whipped. The year before the new President had turned out Maj. Brown and Maj. Cullen, the Indian agents, and put in their places Maj. Galbraith and Mr. Clark Thompson, and they had turned out the men under them and put in others of their own party. There were a great many changes. . . . Nearly all of the men who were turned out were dissatisfied, and most of the Indians did not like the new men. At last Maj. Galbraith went to work about the agencies and recruited a company of soldiers to go South. His men were nearly all half-breeds. This was the company called the Renville Rangers, for they were mostly from Renville County. The Indians now thought the whites [in the North] must be pretty hard up for men to fight the South, or they would not come so far out on the frontier and take half-breeds or anything to help them.

It began to be whispered about that now would be a good time to go to war with the whites and get back the lands. It was believed that the men who had enlisted last had all left the state, and that before help could be sent the Indians could clean out the country, and that the Winnebagoes,[11] and even the Chippewas,[12] would assist the Sioux. It was also thought that a war with the whites would cause the Sioux to forget the troubles among themselves and enable many of them to pay off some old scores.

---

[9] half-breeds—an offensive term for people of mixed Indian and white parentage.

[10] Fort Snelling—United States' Army fort built in 1819 where the Mississippi and Minnesota rivers join.

[11] Winnebagoes—an Indian people originally inhabiting eastern Wisconsin who had been forced to sell their ancestral lands in 1827 and to move to a series of reservations.

[12] Chippewas—also known as the Ojibwas, traditional enemies of the Sioux. They inhabited a large area near Lake Superior in northern Minnesota. In 1815, they had been forced to sell most of their land to the United States government.

Though I took part in the war, I was against it. I knew there was no good cause for it, and I had been to Washington and knew the power of the whites and that they would finally conquer us. We might succeed for a time, but we would be overpowered and defeated at last. I said all this and many more things to my people, but many of my own bands were against me, and some of the other chiefs put words in their mouths to say to me. When the outbreak came Little Crow told some of my band that if I refused to lead them to shoot me as a traitor who would not stand up for his nation, and then select another leader in my place.

But after the first talk of war the **counsels**[13] of the peace Indians prevailed, and many of us thought the danger had all blown over. The time of the government payment was near at hand, and this may have had something to do with it.

There was another thing that helped to stop the war talk. The crops that had been put in by the "farmer" Indians were looking well, and there seemed to be a good prospect for a plentiful supply of provisions for them the coming winter without having to depend on the game of the country or without going far out into the west on the plains for buffalo. It seemed as if the white men's way was certainly the best. Many of the Indians had been short of provisions that summer and had exhausted their credits and were in bad condition. "Now," said the farmer Indians, "if you had worked last season you would not be starving now and begging for food."

The "farmers" were favored by the government in every way. They had houses built for them, some of them even had brick houses, and they were not allowed to suffer. The other Indians did not like this. They were envious of them and jealous, and disliked them because

---

[13] **counsels**—advice.

they had gone back on the customs of the tribe and because they were favored. They called them "farmers," as if it was disgraceful to be a farmer. They called them "cut-hairs," because they had given up the Indian fashion of wearing their hair, and "breeches men," because they wore **pantaloons**,[14] and "Dutchmen," because so many of the settlers on the north side of the river and elsewhere in the country were Germans.[15] I have heard that there was a secret organization of the Indians called the "Soldiers' Lodge," whose object was to declare war against the whites, but I knew nothing of it.

At last the time for the payment came and the Indians came in to the agencies to get their money. But the paymaster did not come, and week after week went by and still he did not come. The payment was to be in gold. Somebody told the Indians that the payment would never be made. The government was in a great war, and gold was scarce, and paper money had taken its place, and it was said the gold could not be had to pay us. Then the trouble began again and the war talk started up. Many of the Indians who had gathered about the agencies were out of provisions and were easily made angry. Still, most of us thought the trouble would pass, and we said nothing about it. I thought there might be trouble, but I had no idea there would be such a war. Little Crow and other chiefs did not think so. But it seems some of the tribe were getting ready for it.

You know how the war started—by the killing of some white people near Acton, in Meeker County. I will tell you how this was done, as it was told me by all of the four young men who did the killing. These young fellows all belonged to Shakopee's band. . . . They told me they did not go out to kill white people. They said

---

[14] **pantaloons**—pants.

[15] Germans in the early United States were often called Dutch from the German word for Germans, *Deutsch*.

they went over into the Big Woods to hunt; that on Sunday, Aug. 17 [1864], they came to a settler's fence, and here they found a hen's nest with some eggs in it. One of them took the eggs, when another said: "Don't take them, for they belong to a white man and we may get into trouble."

The other was angry, for he was very hungry and wanted to eat the eggs, and he dashed them to the ground and replied: "You are a coward. You are afraid of the white man. You are afraid to take even an egg from him, though you are half-starved. Yes, you are a coward, and I will tell everybody so."

The other replied: "I am not a coward. I am not afraid of the white man, and to show you that I am not I will go to the house and shoot him. Are you brave enough to go with me?"

The one who had called him a coward said: "Yes, I will go with you, and we will see who is the braver of us two."

Their two companions then said: "We will go with you, and we will be brave, too." They all went to the house of the white man [Mr. Robinson Jones], but he got alarmed and went to the house [of his son-in-law, Howard Baker], where there were some other white men and women. The four Indians followed them and killed three men and two women [Jones, Baker, a Mr. Webster, Mrs. Jones, and a girl of fourteen]. Then they hitched up a team belonging to another settler and drove to Shakopee's camp [six miles above Redwood agency], which they reached late that night and told what they had done, as I have related.

The tale told by the young men created the greatest excitement. Everybody was waked up and heard it. Shakopee took the young men to Little Crow's house [two miles above the agency], and he sat up in bed and listened to their story. He said war was now declared. Blood had been shed, the payment would be stopped, and the whites would take a dreadful vengeance because women had been killed. Wabasha, Wacouta, myself, and others still talked for peace, but nobody would listen to us, and soon the cry was "Kill the whites and kill all these cut-hairs who will not join us."

A council was held and war was declared. Parties formed and dashed away in the darkness to kill settlers. The women began to run bullets and the men to clean their guns. Little Crow gave orders to attack the agency early next morning and to kill all the traders. When the Indians first came to him for counsel and advice he said to them, **tauntingly**:[16] "Why do you come to me for advice? Go to the man you elected speaker (Traveling Hail) and let him tell you what to do"; but he soon came around all right and somehow took the lead in everything, though he was not head chief, as I have said.

At this time my village was upon Crow Creek, near Little Crow's. I did not have a very large band—not more than thirty or forty fighting men. Most of them were not for the war at first, but nearly all got into it at last. A great many members of the other bands were like my men; they took no part in the first movements, but afterward did. The next morning, when the force started down to attack the agency, I went along. I did not lead my band, and I took no part in the killing. I went to save the lives of two particular friends if I could. I think others went for the same reason, for nearly every Indian had a friend that he did not want killed; of course he did not care about anybody else's friend.

The killing was nearly all done when I got there. Little Crow was on the ground directing operations. The day before, he had attended church there and listened closely to the sermon and had shaken hands with everybody. So many Indians have lied about their saving the lives of white people that I dislike to speak of what I did.

---

[16] **tauntingly**—mockingly, insultingly; in a manner designed to provoke.

But I did save the life of George H. Spencer at the time of the massacre. . . . Once after that I kept a half-breed family from being murdered; these are all the people whose lives I claim to have saved.

I was never present when the white people were willfully murdered. I saw all the dead bodies at the agency. Mr. Andrew Myrick, a trader, with an Indian wife, had refused some hungry Indians credit a short time before when they asked him for some provisions. He said to them: "Go and eat grass." Now he was lying on the ground dead, with his mouth stuffed full of grass, and the Indians were saying tauntingly: "Myrick is eating grass himself."

When I returned to my village that day I found that many of my band had changed their minds about the war, and wanted to get into it. All the other villages were the same way. I was still of the belief that it was not best, but I thought I must go with my band and my nation, and I said to my men that I would lead them into the war, and we would all act like brave Dakotas and do the best we could. All my men were with me; none had gone off on raids, but we did not have guns for all at first.

That afternoon word came to my village that (Capt. Marsh and his men) were coming to the agency from Fort Snelling. At once I mounted the best horse I had, and, with some of my men, rode as fast as I could to meet them at the ferry. But when I got there the fight was over, and I well remember that a cloud of powder smoke was rising slowly from the low, wet ground where the firing had been. I heard a few scattering shots down the river, where the Indians were still pursuing the soldiers, but I took no part. I crossed the river and saw the bodies of the soldiers that had been killed. I think Mr. Quinn, the interpreter, was shot several times after he had been killed. The Indians told me that most of them who fired on Capt. Marsh and his men were on the same side of the river; that only a few shots came from the opposite or south side. They said that White Dog did not tell Mr. Quinn to come over, but told him to go back. Of course I do not know what the truth is about this. White Dog was the Indian head farmer who had been replaced by Taopi and who was hanged at Mankato.

I was not in the first fight at New Ulm nor the first attack on Fort Ridgely. . . . I was in the second fight at New Ulm and in the second attack on Fort Ridgely. At New Ulm I had but a few of my band with me. We lost none of them. We had but few, if any, of the Indians killed; at least I did not hear of but a few. A half-breed named George Le Blanc, who was with us, was killed. There was no one in chief command of the Indians at New Ulm. A few sub-chiefs, like myself, and the head soldiers led them, and the leaders agreed among themselves what was to be done. I do not think there was a chief present at the first fight. I think that attack was made by **marauding**[17] Indians from several bands, every man for himself, but when we heard they were fighting we went down to help them. I think it probable that the first attack on Fort Ridgely was made in the same way. . . .

The second fight at Fort Ridgely was made a grand affair. Little Crow was with us. Mr. Good Thunder, now at Birch Coulie agency, was with us. He counted the Indians as they filed past him on the march to the attack, and reported that there were 800 of us. He acted very bravely in the fight, and distinguished himself by running close up to the fort and bringing away a horse. He is now married to the former widow of White Dog, and both he and his wife are good Christian citizens. We went down determined to take the fort, for we knew it was of the greatest importance to us to have it. If we could take it we would soon have the whole Minnesota valley. But we failed, and of course it was best that we did fail.

---

[17] **marauding**—roving and raiding in search of booty.

Though Little Crow was present, he did not take a very active part in the fight. As I remember, the chief leaders in the fight were "The Thief," who was the head soldier of Mankato's band, and Mankato himself. He was a very brave man and a good leader. We went down to the attack on both sides of the river. I went down on the south side with my men, and we crossed the river in front of the fort and went up through the timber and fought on that side next [to] the river. The fight **commenced**[18] about noon on Friday after the outbreak. We had a few Sissetons and Wakpatons with us, and some Winnebagoes, under the "Little Priest," were in this fight and at New Ulm. I saw them myself.

But for the cannon, I think we would have taken the fort. The soldiers fought us so bravely we thought there were more of them than there were. The cannons disturbed us greatly, but did not hurt many. We did not have many Indians killed. I think the whites put the number too large, and I think they overestimated the number killed in every battle. We seldom carried off our dead. We usually buried them in a secluded place on the battlefield when we could. We always tried to carry away the wounded.

When we retreated from Ridgely I recrossed the river opposite the fort and went up on the south side. All our army but the scouts fell back[19] up the river to other villages near Redwood agency, and then on up to the Yellow Medicine and the mouth of the Chippewa. Our scouts brought word that our old friend Wapetonhonska ("The Long Trader"), as we called Gen. Sibley, was coming up against us, and in a few days we learned that he had come to Fort Ridgely with a large number of soldiers.

Little Crow, with a strong party, went over into the Big Woods, towards Forest City and Hutchinson. After he had gone, I and the other sub-chiefs concluded to go

---

[18] **commenced**—began.

[19] fell back—retreated.

down and attack New Ulm again and take the town and cross the river to the east, or in the rear of Fort Ridgely, where Sibley was, and then our movements were to be governed by circumstances.

We had left our village near the Redwood in some haste and alarm, expecting to be followed after the defeat at Ridgely, and had not taken all our property away. So we took many of our women with us to gather up the property and some other things, and we brought along some wagons to haul them off. We came down the main road on the south side of the river, and were several hundred strong. We left our camps in the morning and got to our old villages in the afternoon.

When the men in advance reached Little Crow's village—which was on the high bluff on the south side of the Minnesota, below the mouth of the Redwood—they looked to the north across the valley, and tip of the high bluff on the north side, and out on the prairie some miles away, they saw a column of mounted men and some wagons coming out of the Beaver Creek timber on the prairie and going eastward. We also saw signs in Little Crow's village that white men had been there only a few hours before, and judging from the trail they had made when they left, these were the men we now saw to the northward.

There was, of course, a little excitement, and the column halted. Four or five of our best scouts were sent across the valley to follow the movements of the soldiers, creeping across the prairie like so many ants. It was near sundown, and we knew they would soon go into camp, and we thought the camping ground would be somewhere on the Birch Coulie,[20] where there was wood and water. The women went to work to load the wagons. The scouts followed the soldiers carefully, and a little after sundown returned with the information that they had

---

[20] Coulie—deep ravine, usually spelled *coulee*.

gone into camp near the head of Birch Coulie. At this time we did not know there were two companies there. We thought the company of mounted men (Capt. Anderson's) was all, and that there were not more than seventy-five men.

It was concluded to surround the camp that night and attack it at daylight. We felt sure we could capture it, and that 200 men would be enough for the undertaking. So about that number was selected. There were four bands—my own, Red Legs', Gray Bird's, and Mankato's. I had about thirty men. Nearly all the Indians had double-barreled shotguns, and we loaded them with buckshot and large bullets called "traders' balls." After dark we started, crossed the river and valley, went up the bluffs and on the prairie, and soon we saw the white tents and the wagons of the camp. We had no difficulty in surrounding the camp. The **pickets**[21] were only a little way from it. I led my men up from the west through the grass and took up a position 200 yards from the camp, behind a small knoll or elevation. Red Legs took his men into the coulie east of the camp. Mankato had some of his men in the coulie and some on the prairie. Gray Bird and his men were mostly on the prairie.

Just at dawn the fight began. It continued all day and the following night until late the next morning. Both sides fought well. Owing to the white men's way of fighting they lost many men. Owing to the Indians' way of fighting they lost but few. The white men stood up and exposed themselves at first, but at last they learned to keep quiet. The Indians always took care of themselves. We had an easy time of it. We could crawl through the grass and into the coulie and get water when we wanted it, and after a few hours our women crossed the river and came up near the bluff and cooked

---

[21] **pickets**—military detachment advanced to warn of an enemy's approach.

for us, and we could go back and eat and then return to the fight.

We did not lose many men. Indeed, I only saw two dead Indians, and I never heard that any more were killed. The two I saw were in the coulie and belonged to Red Legs' band. One was a Wakpaton and the other was a Sisseton. Their bodies were taken down the coulie and buried during the fight. I did not see a man killed on the prairie. We had several men wounded, but none very badly. . . .

About the middle of the afternoon our men became much dissatisfied at the slowness of the fight, and the stubbornness of the whites, and the word was passed around the lines to get ready to charge the camp. The brave Mankato wanted to charge after the first hour.

There were some half-breeds with the whites who could speak Sioux well, and they heard us arranging to assault them. One told me afterward that he heard us talking about it very plainly. Another who was there and heard the talk called out to us: "You do very wrong to fire on us. We did not come out to fight; we only came out to bury the bodies of the white people you killed." I have heard that these men and another half-breed dug a **rifle pit**[22] for themselves with bayonets, and that one worked so hard with his bayonet in digging that he wore the flesh from the inside of his hand. One half-breed attempted to desert to us, but as he was running towards us some of our men shot and killed him. We could have taken the camp, I think. During the fight the whites had thrown up **breastworks**,[23] but they were not very high and we could easily have jumped over them. . . .

Just as we were about to charge word came that a large number of mounted soldiers were coming up from

---

[22] **rifle pit**—hole large enough for one man to take cover.

[23] **breastworks**—quickly dug fortification consisting of a trench in which the dirt is piled up "breast high" on the side from which the attack is expected.

the east toward Fort Ridgely. This stopped the charge and created some excitement. Mankato at once took some men from the coulie and went out to meet them. He told me he did not take more than fifty, but he scattered them out and they all yelled and made such a noise that the whites must have thought there were a great many more, and they stopped on the prairie and began fighting. The [United States] soldiers had a cannon and used it, but it did no harm. If the Indians had any men killed in the fight I never heard of it. Mankato flourished his men around so, and all the Indians in the coulie kept up a noise, and at last the whites began to fall back, and they retreated about two miles and began to dig breastworks. Mankato followed them and left about thirty men to watch them, and returned to the fight at the coulie with the rest. The Indians were laughing when they came back at the way they had deceived the white men, and we were all glad that the whites had not pushed forward and driven us away.

If any more Indians went against this force than the fifty or possibly seventy-five that I have told you of I never heard of it. I was not with them and cannot say positively, but I do not think there were. I went out to near the fortified camp during the night, and there was no large force of Indians over there, and I know there were not more than thirty of our men watching the camp. When the men of this force began to fall back, the whites in the camp **hallooed**[24] and made a great commotion, as if they were begging them to return and relieve them, and seemed much distressed that they did not.

The next morning Gen. Sibley came with a very large force and drove us away from the field. We took our time about getting away. Some of our men said they remained till Sibley got up and that they fired at some of his men as they were shaking hands with some of the

---

[24] **hallooed**—shouted loudly with the intent of attracting attention.

men of the camp. Those of us who were on the prairie went back to the westward and on down the valley. Those in the coulie went down back southward to where their horses were, and then mounted and rode westward across the prairie about a mile south of the battlefield. There was no pursuit. The whites fired their cannons at us as we were leaving the field, but they might as well have beaten a big drum for all the harm they did. They only made a noise. We went back across the river to our camps in the old villages, and then on up the river to the Yellow Medicine and the mouth of the Chippewa, where Little Crow joined us.

For some time after the fight at Birch Coulie the greater part of the Indians remained in the camps about the Yellow Medicine and the mouth of the Chippewa. At last the word came that Sibley with his army was again on the move against us. Our scouts were very active and vigilant, and we heard from them nearly every hour.

He [Sibley] had left a letter for Little Crow in a split stick on the battlefield of Birch Coulie, and some of our men found it and brought it in, and correspondence had been going on between us ever since. . . . I and others understood that Gen. Sibley would treaty with all of us who had only been soldiers and would surrender as prisoners of war, and that only those who had murdered people in cold blood, the settlers and others, would be punished in any way. There was great dissatisfaction among us at our condition. Many wanted to surrender, others left us for the West. But Sibley came on and on, and at last came the battle of Wood Lake.

When we learned that Sibley had gone into camp at the Wood Lake, a council of the sub-chiefs and others was held and it was determined to give him a battle near there. . . . We soon learned that Sibley had thrown up breastworks and it was not deemed safe to attack him at the lake. We concluded that the fight should be about a mile or more to the northwest of the lake, on the road along which the troops would march. This was the road leading to the upper country, and of course Sibley would travel it. At the point determined on we planned to hide a large number of men on the side of the road. Near the lake, in a ravine formed by the outlet, we were to place another strong body. Behind a hill to the west were to be some more men. We thought that when Sibley marched out along the road and when the head of his column had reached the farther end of the line of our first division, our men would open fire. The men in the ravine would then be in the rear of the whites and would begin firing on that end of the column. The men from behind the hill would rush out and attack the flank, and then we had horsemen far out on the right and left who would come up. We expected to throw the whole white force into confusion by the sudden and unexpected attack and defeat them before they could rally.

I think this was a good plan of battle. Our concealed men would not have been discovered. The grass was tall and the place by the road and the ravine were good hiding places. We had learned that Sibley was not particular about sending out scouts and examining the country before he passed it. He had a number of mounted men, but they always rode together, at the head of the columns, when on a march, and did not examine the ground at the sides of the road. The night he lay at Wood Lake his pickets were only a short distance from camp—less than half a mile. When we were putting our men into position that night we often saw them plainly.

I worked hard that night fixing the men. Little Crow was on the field, too. Mankato was there. Indeed, all our fighting chiefs were present and all our best fighting Indians. We felt that this would be the deciding fight of the war. The whites were

unconscious.[25] We could hear them laughing and singing. When all our preparations were made, Little Crow and I and some other chiefs went to the mound or hill to the west so as to watch the fight better when it should commence.

The morning came and an accident spoiled all our plans. For some reason Sibley did not move early as we expected he would. Our men were lying hidden waiting patiently. Some were very near the camp lines in the ravine, but the whites did not see a single man of all our men. I do not think they would have discovered our **ambuscade.**[26] It seemed a considerable time after sun-up when some four or five wagons with a number of soldiers started out from the camp in the direction of the old Yellow Medicine agency. We learned afterwards that they were going without orders to dig potatoes over at the agency, five miles away. They came on over the prairie, right where part of our line was. Some of the wagons were not in the road, and if they had kept straight on would have driven right over our men as they lay in the grass. At last they came so close that our men had to rise up and fire. This brought on the fight, of course, but not according to the way we had planned it. Little Crow saw it and felt very badly.

Of course you know how the battle was fought. The Indians that were in the fight did well, but hundreds of our men did not get into it and did not fire a shot. They were out too far. The men in the ravine and the line connecting them with those on the road did most of the fighting. Those of us on the hill did our best, but we were soon driven off. Mankato was killed here, and we lost a very good and brave war chief. He was killed by a cannon ball that was so nearly spent

---

[25] **unconscious**—as it is used here, the word means that the soldiers were unaware of the presence of the Indians.

[26] **ambuscade**—ambush or surprise attack from a concealed position.

that he was not afraid of it, and it struck him in the back, as he lay on the ground, and killed him. The whites drove our men out of the ravine by a charge and that ended the battle. We retreated in some disorder, though the whites did not offer to pursue us. We crossed a wide prairie, but their horsemen did not follow us. We lost fourteen or fifteen men killed and quite a number wounded. Some of the wounded died afterwards, but I do not know how many. We carried off no dead bodies, but took away all our wounded. The whites scalped all our dead men—so I have heard.

Soon after the battle I, with many others who had taken part in the war, surrendered to Gen. Sibley. Robinson and the other half-breeds assured us that if we would do this we would only be held as prisoners of war a short time, but as soon as I surrendered I was thrown into prison. Afterwards I was tried and served three years in the prison at Davenport and the penitentiary at Rock Island for taking part in the war.

At my trial a great number of the white prisoners, women and others were called up, but not one of them could testify that I had murdered any one or had done anything to deserve death, or else I would have been hanged. If I had known that I would be sent to the penitentiary I would not have surrendered, but when I had been in the penitentiary three years and they were about to turn me out, I told them they might keep me another year if they wished, and I meant what I said. I did not like the way I had been treated. I surrendered in good faith, knowing that many of the whites were acquainted with me and that I had not been a murderer, or present when a murder had been committed, and if I had killed or wounded a man it had been in fair, open fight.

QUESTIONS TO CONSIDER

1. What did the Sioux people hope to gain from the uprising?

2. Why did Big Eagle, the narrator, take part in the uprising? Why did he believe it would succeed?

3. How did the Civil War affect the Sioux leaders' decision making?

4. How, specifically, did the fighting style of the whites and Indians differ?

5. What, in your opinion, seems to be Big Eagle's attitude toward white people? What can you find in his narrative to support your opinion?

Surrender Speech

BY COCHISE (CHIRICAHUA APACHE)

The homeland of the Apache people was located in the southern part of what are now the states of Arizona and New Mexico. In the late 1840s, the United States Army first entered the area and encountered the Chiricahua Apache. For the next forty years, the army attempted to keep the Chiricahuas from attacking white travelers and settlers. Beginning in the 1860s, the great Apache leader Cochise fought off repeated attempts to end his control of southern Arizona. In 1872, after a decade of war, Cochise finally agreed to stop fighting, but not before expressing his resentment about the Indians' loss of freedom and independence. The following speech, made to the white military officers to whom he surrendered, is included in historian W. C. Vanderwerth's 1971 book, Indian Oratory.

"You Must Speak Straight so that Your Words May Go as Sunlight to Our Hearts"

The sun has been very hot on my head and made me as in a fire; my blood was on fire, but now I have come into

---

this valley and drunk of these waters and washed myself in them and they have cooled me. Now that I am cool I have come with my hands open to you to live in peace with you. I speak straight and do not wish to deceive or be deceived. I want a good, strong, and lasting peace.

When God made the world he gave one part to the white man and another to the Apache. Why was it? Why did they come together? Now that I am to speak, the sun, the moon, the earth, the air, the waters, the birds and beasts, even the children unborn, shall rejoice at my words. The white people have looked for me long. I am here! What do they want? They have looked for me long; why am I worth so much? If I am worth so much why not **mark**[1] when I set my foot and look when I spit?

The coyotes go about at night to rob and kill; I can not see them; I am not God. I am no longer chief of all the Apaches. I am no longer rich; I am but a poor man. The world was not always this way. I can not command the animals; if I would they would not obey me. God made us not as you; we were born like the animals, in the dry grass, not on beds like you. This is why we do as the animals, go about . . . [at] night and rob and steal. If I had such things as you have, I would not do as I do, for then I would not need to do so. There are Indians who go about killing and robbing. I do not command them. If I did, they would not do so. My warriors have been killed in Sonora.[2] I came here because God told me to do so. He said it was good to be at peace—so I came! I was going around the world with the clouds, and air, when God spoke to my thought and told me to come in here and be at peace with all. He said the world was for us all; how was it? When I was young I walked all over this country, east and west, and saw no other people than the Apaches. After many summers I walked again and found another race of people had come to take it. How is it? Why is it that the Apaches wait to

---

[1] **mark**—take notice.

[2] Sonora—state in northern Mexico that borders on the southwestern United States.

die—that they carry their lives on their fingernails? They roam over the hills and plains and want the heavens to fall on them. The Apaches were once a great nation; they are now but few, and because of this they want to die and so carry their lives on their fingernails. Many have been killed in battle. You must speak straight so that your words may go as sunlight to our hearts. Tell me, if the Virgin Mary[3] has walked throughout all the land, why has she never entered the wigwam of the Apache? Why have we never seen or heard her?

I have no father or mother; I am alone in the world. No one cares for Cochise; that is why I do not care to live, and wish the rocks to fall on me and cover me up. If I had a father and a mother like you, I would be with them and they with me. When I was going around the world, all were asking for Cochise. Now he is here—you see him and hear him—are you glad? If so, say so. Speak, Americans and Mexicans, I do not wish to hide anything from you nor have you hide anything from me; I will not lie to you; do not lie to me. I want to live in these mountains; I do not want to go to Tularosa.[4] That is a long ways off. The flies on those mountains eat out the eyes of horses. The bad spirits live there. I have drunk of these waters and they have cooled me; I do not want to leave here.

---

[3] Virgin Mary—mother of Jesus Christ, according to the Christian faith, and an especially important religious figure to the Mexican Catholics with whom Cochise would have come in contact.

[4] Tularosa—reservation established by the United States government for a portion of the Apache people. The Tularosa Valley is a poorly drained area that lies between the Sacramento and San Andres mountains in southern New Mexico.

QUESTIONS TO CONSIDER

1. What mood does Cochise express in his statement?

2. According to Cochise, what are the differences between the white and the Apache people?

3. What does Cochise ask the whites to do? Why does he make this request?

Resistance

Cochise Cochise, who became principal chief of the Apaches in 1863, took to the warpath after several of his relatives were hanged by an Army officer. He and 200 followers eluded capture for more than ten years by hiding out in the Dragoon Mountains of Arizona, from which they continued their raids. Cochise surrendered but escaped in the spring of 1872. He surrendered again when the Chiricahua Reservation was established that summer, and there he died on June 8, 1874.

▲
Part of the Black Hawk War, this battle took place at Bad Ax on August 1 and 2, 1832.

Seminole Wars From 1835 to 1842, the Seminole Indians resisted all attempts to remove them from Florida. Future President Zachary Taylor won a promotion based on his leadership in the battle pictured here, which took place December 25, 1837.
▼

In 1874, some 4,000 Apaches were forcibly moved to a reservation at San Carlos, Arizona, where they revolted. Spurred by their leader, Geronimo, hundreds of Apaches left the reservation to resume their war against the whites. Geronimo surrendered in January 1884, but escaped in May 1885. Nearly a year later, Geronimo surrendered in Mexico, but escaped before reaching American soil. In 1886, Geronimo surrendered for the last time, lured by false promises that his people could return to their land. He never saw Arizona again and died at Fort Sill, Oklahoma, on February 17, 1909.

▲
Chief Geronimo.

Background Geronimo with warriors.

Chief Joseph of the Nez Percé was born in Oregon in 1840 and became chief upon the death of his father in 1871. A federal order banned white settlers from their territory in 1873, but in 1877 the cavalry threatened to attack if Joseph didn't lead his people to a reservation in Idaho. Reluctantly he agreed; however, when a small band of Nez Percé warriors led a raid on nearby white settlers, the army began to pursue Joseph. Before his surrender in October 1877, Joseph led a brilliant campaign against the much bigger army forces. The Nez Percé were moved to Kansas, then Oklahoma, and finally returned to the Pacific Northwest in 1885.

Young Joseph.
▼

◀ Sketch of Chief Joseph.

Wagon train attack.
▼

▲

Chief Joseph in ceremonial dress.

Chapter 4

Destruction by Policy and Practice

The Iroquois and the American Revolution

BY MARY JEMISON

During the 1700s, the combination of disease and warfare greatly reduced the population of the powerful Iroquois tribes of upstate New York. As a result, the Iroquois developed the practice of sometimes adopting white and Indian captives in order to sustain their tribes. Mary Jemison, a white woman, was captured and adopted into the Seneca tribe, one of the six Iroquois nations. Many of these so-called white Indians freely accepted their new lives and showed no interest in returning to their families. Mary spent the rest of her life with the Senecas, and many of her Seneca descendants carry on the Jemison name in the tribe to this day. Mary Jemison lived during the American Revolution (1775–83), when her adopted people were forced to choose between supporting the British or the American side. Her account tells of the difficult decisions and the terrible hardships the Iroquois people suffered, largely at the hands of American soldiers.

Thus, at peace amongst themselves, and with the neighboring whites, though there were none at that time very near, our Indians lived quietly and peaceably at home, till a little before the breaking out of the revolutionary war, when they were sent for, together with the Chiefs and members of the Six Nations[1] generally, by the people of the States, to go to the German Flats, and there hold a general council, in order that the people of the states might **ascertain**,[2] in good season, who they should esteem and treat as enemies, and who as friends, in the great war which was then upon the point of breaking out between them and the King of England.

Our Indians obeyed the call, and the council was holden, at which the pipe of peace was smoked, and a treaty made, in which the Six Nations solemnly agreed that if a war should eventually break out, they would not take up arms on either side; but that they would observe a strict **neutrality**.[3] With that the people of the states were satisfied, as they had not asked their assistance, nor did not wish it. The Indians returned to their homes well pleased that they could live on neutral ground, surrounded by the **din**[4] of war, without being engaged in it.

About a year passed off, and we, as usual, were enjoying ourselves in the employments of peaceable times, when a messenger arrived from the British Commissioners, requesting all the Indians of our tribe to attend a general council which was soon to be held at Oswego.[5] The council convened, and being opened, the British Commissioners informed the Chiefs that the

---

[1] Six Nations—the six tribes that make up the Iroquois nation: Oneida, Onondaga, Cayuga, Seneca, Tuscarora, and Mohawk. The tribes lived in northern New York state and Canada.

[2] **ascertain**—discover with certainty.

[3] **neutrality**—refusal to support either of the two sides engaged in a war or dispute.

[4] **din**—loud continuous noise.

[5] Oswego—a British fort located on the shores of Lake Ontario in western New York state.

object of calling a council of the Six Nations, was to engage their assistance in subduing the rebels, the people of the states, who had risen up against the good King, their master, and were about to rob him of a great part of his possessions and wealth, and added that they would amply reward them for all their services.

The Chiefs then arose, and informed the Commissioners of the nature and extent of the treaty which they had entered into with the people of the states, the year before, and that they should not violate it by taking up the hatchet[6] against them.

The Commissioners continued their **entreaties**[7] without success, till they addressed their **avarice**,[8] by telling our people that the people of the states were few in number, and easily subdued; and that on the account of their disobedience to the King, they justly merited all the punishment that it was possible for white men and Indians to inflict upon them; and added, that the King was rich and powerful, both in money and subjects: that his rum was as plenty as the water in lake Ontario; that his men were as numerous as the sands upon the lake shore—and that the Indians, if they should assist in the war, and persevere in their friendship to the King, till it was closed, should never want for money or goods. Upon this the Chiefs concluded a treaty with the British Commissioners, in which they agreed to take up arms against the rebels, and continue in the service of his Majesty till they were subdued, in consideration of certain conditions which were **stipulated**[9] in the treaty to be performed by the British government and its agents.

As soon as the treaty was finished, the Commissioners made a present to each Indian of a suit of clothes, a brass kettle, a gun and a tomahawk, a scalping knife, a quantity

---

[6] taking up the hatchet—an Iroquois expression meaning "to go to war."

[7] **entreaties**—pleas or requests.

[8] **avarice**—greed.

[9] **stipulated**—stated conditions or terms (of a treaty or agreement).

of powder and lead, a piece of gold, and promised a bounty on every scalp that should be brought in. Thus richly clad and equipped, they returned home, after an absence of about two weeks, full of the fire of war, and anxious to encounter their enemies. . . .

Previous to the battle at Fort Stanwix,[10] the British sent for the Indians to come and see them whip the rebels; and, at the same time stated that they did not wish to have them fight, but wanted to have them just sit down, smoke their pipes, and look on. Our Indians went, to a man; but contrary to their expectation, instead of smoking and looking on, they were obliged to fight for their lives, and in the end of the battle were completely beaten, with a great loss killed and wounded. Our Indians alone had thirty-six killed, and a great number wounded. Our town exhibited a scene of real sorrow and distress, when our warriors returned and recounted their misfortunes, and stated the real loss they had sustained in the engagement. The mourning was excessive, and was expressed by the most **doleful**[11] yells, shrieks, and howlings, and by inimitable gesticulations.[12]

During the revolution, my house was the home of Col's Butler and Brandt,[13] whenever they chanced to come into our neighborhood as they passed to and from Fort Niagara,[14] which was the seat of their military operations. Many and many a night I have pounded samp[15] for them from sunset till sunrise, and furnished them

---

[10] In this 1777 battle in western New York, both British and American troops had Iroquois allies on their side. Many Iroquois warriors lost their lives in this American victory.

[11] **doleful**—expressing grief; mournful.

[12] inimitable gesticulations—gestures that cannot be imitated.

[13] Col's Butler and Brandt—Colonel John Butler commanded a regiment of Tory troops (Americans who remained loyal to the British during the American Revolution) and Iroquois Indians. Colonel Joseph Brandt was a Mohawk chief who had been educated in England and also commanded Tory and Indian troops during the war.

[14] Fort Niagara—British fort located between Lake Ontario and Lake Erie in western New York.

[15] samp—cornmeal, usually made into a porridge like oatmeal.

with necessary provision and clean clothing for their journey. . . .

At that time I had three children who went with me on foot, one who rode on horseback, and one whom I carried on my back.

Our corn was good that year; a part of which we had gathered and secured for winter.

In one or two days after the skirmish at Connissius Lake, Sullivan[16] and his army arrived at Genesee river, where they destroyed every article of the food kind that they could lay their hands on. A part of our corn they burnt, and threw the remainder into the river. They burnt our houses, killed what few cattle and horses they could find, destroyed our fruit trees, and left nothing but the bare soil and timber. But the Indians had eloped[17] and were not to be found.

Having crossed and recrossed the river, and finished the work of destruction, the army marched off to the east. Our Indians saw them move off, but suspecting that it was Sullivan's intention to watch our return, and then to take us by surprise, resolved that the main body of our tribe should hunt where we then were, till Sullivan had gone so far that there would be no danger of his returning to molest us.

This being agreed to, we hunted continually till the Indians concluded that there could be no risk in our once more taking possession of our lands. Accordingly we all returned; but what were our feelings when we found that there was not a mouthful of any kind of **sustenance**[18] left, not even enough to keep a child one day from perishing with hunger.

---

[16] Sullivan—General John Sullivan commanded an army of 4,000 American troops. In 1779, under orders from General George Washington, Sullivan's army destroyed more than forty Iroquois villages and ended the influence of the Six Nations.

[17] eloped—run away.

[18] **sustenance**—food on which to survive.

The weather by this time had become cold and stormy; and as we were destitute of houses and food too, I immediately resolved to take my children and look out for myself, without delay. With this intention I took two of my little ones on my back, **bade**[19] the other three follow, and the same night arrived on the Gardow flats, where I have ever since resided. . . .

. . . The snow fell about five feet deep, and remained so for a long time, and the weather was extremely cold; so much so indeed, that almost all the game upon which the Indians depended for subsistence, perished, and reduced them almost to a state of starvation through that and three or four succeeding years. When the snow melted in the spring, deer were found dead upon the ground in vast numbers; and other animals, of every description, perished from the cold also, and were found dead, in multitudes. Many of our people barely escaped with their lives, and some actually died of hunger and freezing.

---

[19] **bade**—directed that.

QUESTIONS TO CONSIDER

1. What decision did the chiefs and members of the Six Nations have to make when they met at the German Flats at the beginning of the Revolution? What did they decide?

2. What promises did the British commissioners make to the Six Nations at the general council at Oswego? Were the British able to keep their promise?

3. What did the American troops under General Sullivan do to the Six Nations' villages and fields?

4. What was the result of the decisions that the Six Nations made during the American Revolution?

The Cherokee Removal

BY CHEROKEE WOMEN
AND REBECCA NEUGIN (CHEROKEE)

*In an effort to better coexist with whites, the Cherokee people of
the Carolinas and Georgia had transformed their way of life, adopting
white methods of commercial agriculture and establishing law
courts, schools, and a written form of their own language. However,
the death of the Seneca chief Tecumseh while fighting for the British
in the War of 1812, and the collapse of his alliance, left the Indians
of the southeastern United States in an increasingly vulnerable
position. After years of debate, President Andrew Jackson responded
to white political pressure and ordered the Cherokees removed from
their homeland. The Cherokees were led westward by United States
soldiers to reservations in the Oklahoma Territory during the winter
of 1838–39, after Jackson had left office. This infamous journey,
known as the "Trail of Tears," saw nearly 13,000 Cherokees driven
from their homes. Along the journey about 4,000 people died of
hunger, exposure, and disease. The following selections include
petitions from Cherokee women during the years leading up to the*

From *The Fighting Cheyennes* by George Bird Grinnell. Reprinted by permission
of University of Oklahoma Press.

removal and a recollection of a Cherokee woman who was three years old when her family made the difficult trek to Oklahoma.

Cherokee Women Petition
May 2, 1817

The Cherokee ladies now being present at the meeting of the chiefs and warriors in council have thought it their duty as mothers to address their beloved chiefs and warriors now assembled.

Our beloved children and head men[1] of the Cherokee Nation, we address you warriors in council. We have raised all of you on the land which we now have, which God gave us to inhabit and raise provisions. We know that our country has once been extensive, but by repeated sales has become **circumscribed**[2] to a small track, and [we] never have thought it our duty to interfere in the disposition of it till now. If a father or mother was to sell all their lands which they had to depend on, which their children had to raise their living on, which would be indeed bad & to be removed to another country. We do not wish to go to an unknown country [to] which we have understood some of our children wish to go over the Mississippi, but this act of our children would be like destroying your mothers.

Your mothers, your sisters ask and beg of you not to part with any more of our land. We say ours. You are our descendants; take pity on our request. But keep it for our growing children, for it was the good will of our creator to place us here, and you know our father, the great president,[3] will not allow his white children to take our country away. Only keep your hands off of paper talks[4] for it's our own country. For [if] it was not, they would not ask you to put your hands to paper, for it would be

---

[1] head men—chiefs.

[2] **circumscribed**—restricted or confined.

[3] the great president—James Monroe, president of the United States (1817–25).

[4] paper talks—written contracts or agreements; treaties.

impossible to remove us all. For as soon as one child is raised, we have others in our arms, for such is our situation & will consider our circumstance.

Therefore, children, don't part with any more of our lands but continue on it & enlarge your farms. Cultivate and raise corn & cotton and your mothers and sisters will make clothing for you which our father the president has recommended to us all. We don't charge any body for selling any lands, but we have heard such intentions of our children. But your talks become true at last; it was our desire to forewarn you all not to part with our lands.

Nancy Ward to her children: Warriors do take pity and listen to the talks of your sisters. Although I am very old, yet I cannot but pity the situation in which you will hear of their minds. I have [a] great many grandchildren which [I] wish them to do well on our land.

Cherokee Women Petition
June 30, 1818

Beloved Children,

We have called a meeting among ourselves to consult on the different points now before the council, relating to our national affairs. We have heard with painful feelings that the bounds of the land we now possess are to be drawn into very narrow limits. The land was given to us by the Great Spirit above as our common right, to raise our children upon, & to make support for our rising generations. We therefore humbly petition our beloved children, the head men & warriors, to hold out to the last in support of our common rights, as the Cherokee nation have been the first settlers of this land; we therefore claim the right of the soil.

We well remember that our country was formerly very extensive, but by repeated sales it has become circumscribed to the very narrow limits we have at present. Our Father the President advised us to become farmers, to manufacture our own clothes, & to have our children instructed. To this advice we have attended in every thing as far as we were able. Now the thought of being compelled to remove to the other side of the Mississippi is dreadful to us, because it appears to us that we, by this removal, shall be brought to a savage state again, for we have, by the endeavor of our Father the President, become too much enlightened to throw aside the privileges of a civilized life.

We therefore unanimously join in our meeting to hold our country in common as hitherto.[5]

Some of our children have become Christians. We have missionary schools among us. We have heard the gospel in our nation. We have become civilized & enlightened, & are in hopes that in a few years our nation will be prepared for instruction in other branches of sciences & arts, which are both useful & necessary in civilized society.

There are some white men among us who have been raised in this country from their youth, are connected with us by marriage, & have considerable families, who are very active in encouraging the emigration of our nation. They ought to be our truest friends but prove our worst enemies. They seem to be only concerned how to increase their riches, but do not care what becomes of our Nation, nor even of their own wives and children.

Cherokee Women Petition
October 17, 1831

To the Committee and Council,

We the females, residing in Salequoree and Pine Log, believing that the present difficulties and embarrassments under which this nation is placed demands a full expression of the mind of every individual on the subject of emigrating to Arkansas [actually, Oklahoma], would

[5] hitherto—before.

take upon ourselves to address you. Although it is not common for our sex to take part in public measures, we nevertheless feel justified in expressing our sentiments on any subject where our interest is as much at stake as any other part of the community.

We believe the present plan of the General Government to effect our removal West of the Mississippi, and thus obtain our lands for the use of the State of Georgia, to be highly oppressive, cruel and unjust. And we sincerely hope there is no consideration which can induce our citizens to forsake the land of our fathers of which they have been in possession from **time immemorial**,[6] and thus compel us, against our will, to undergo the toils and difficulties of removing[7] with our helpless families hundreds of miles to [an] unhealthy and unproductive country. We hope therefore the Committee and Council will take into deep consideration our **deplorable**[8] situation, and do everything in their power to **avert**[9] such a state of things. And we trust by a **prudent**[10] course their transactions with the General Government will enlist in our behalf the sympathies of the good people of the United States.

Recollections of Removal
by Rebecca Neugin

When the soldiers came to our house my father wanted to fight, but my mother told him that the soldiers would kill him if he did and we surrendered without a fight. They drove us out of our house to join other prisoners in a stockade. After they took us away my mother begged them to let her go back and get some bedding. So they let her go back and she brought what

---

[6] **time immemorial**—all of traditional and recorded history.

[7] removing—going out.

[8] **deplorable**—worthy of severe condemnation; lamentable; wretched, bad.

[9] **avert**—turn away; prevent.

[10] **prudent**—wise and careful in practical matters.

bedding and a few cooking utensils she could carry and had to leave behind all of our other household possessions. My father had a wagon pulled by two spans[11] of oxen to haul us in. Eight of my brothers and sisters and two or three widow women and children rode with us. My brother Dick who was a good deal older than I was walked along with a long whip which he popped over the backs of the oxen and drove them all the way. My father and mother walked all the way also. The people got so tired of eating salt pork on the journey that my father would walk through the woods as we traveled, hunting for turkeys and deer which he brought into camp to feed us. Camp was usually made at some place where water was to be had and when we stopped and prepared to cook our food other emigrants who had been driven from their homes without opportunity to secure cooking utensils came to our camp to use our pots and kettles. There was much sickness among the emigrants and a great many little children died of whooping cough.

---

[11] spans—harnessed teams.

QUESTIONS TO CONSIDER

1. In the first two petitions, what do the Cherokee women see as the greatest threat to their homeland?

2. How does the attitude of the Cherokee women toward whites change over time?

3. How do the Cherokee women justify their right to express their opinions and be heard?

4. According to the women, what hardships will the Cherokee people suffer if they are removed from their homeland?

5. What, in your opinion, were the worst hardships the Cherokee people faced on the trek to Oklahoma?

6. What do you think they must have endured once they arrived on the reservation in Oklahoma?

The Sand Creek Massacre

BY GEORGE BENT (CHEYENNE)

The 1864 Sand Creek Massacre stands as one of the most infamous single examples of white injustice and brutality against Native Americans. A group of Cheyenne people led by Black Kettle had avoided war and removed themselves to the barren land around Sand Creek in southeastern Colorado. Here they thought they would be safe under the protection of the American flag. George Bent, a trader who was part Cheyenne himself, witnessed the massacre and left the following account. Even in an era when most Americans had little tolerance or sympathy for Indian people, many were appalled by the cruelty of the Sand Creek Massacre. This led to the first Congressional investigation into American Indian policy. While the government's overall policies were called into question, none of the white participants in the Sand Creek Massacre was ever punished.

When I looked toward the chief's lodge, I saw that Black Kettle[1] had a large American flag up on a long lodgepole as a signal to the troop that the camp was friendly. Part of the warriors were running out toward the pony herds and the rest of the people were rushing about the camp in great fear. All the time Black Kettle kept calling out not to be frightened; that the camp was under protection and there was no danger. Then suddenly the troops opened fire on this mass of men, women, and children, and all began to scatter and run.

The main body of Indians rushed up the bed of the creek, which was dry, level sand with only a few little pools of water here and there. On each side of this wide bed stood banks from two to ten feet high. While the main body of the people fled up this dry bed, a part of the young men were trying to save the herd from the soldiers, and small parties were running in all directions toward the sand hills. One of these parties, made up of perhaps ten middle-aged Cheyenne men, started for the sand hills west of the creek, and I joined them. Before we had gone far, the troops saw us and opened a heavy fire on us, forcing us to run back and take shelter in the bed of the creek. We now started up the stream bed, following the main body of Indians and with a whole company of cavalry close on our heels shooting at us every foot of the way. As we went along we passed many Indians, men, women, and children, some wounded, others dead, lying on the sand and in the pools of water. Presently we came to a place where the main party had stopped, and were now hiding in pits that they had dug in the high bank of the stream. Just as we reached this place, I was struck by a ball in the hip and badly wounded, but I managed to get into one of the pits. About these

---

[1] Black Kettle—chief of the southern Cheyenne people. He had always advocated peaceful relations with whites and avoided violence at all costs. Black Kettle had notified the United States soldiers at nearby Fort Lyon that he was camped at Sand Creek and was led to believe that his people were safe.

pits nearly all Chivington's men[2] had gathered and more were continually coming up, for they had given up the pursuit of the small bodies of Indians who had fled to the sand hills.

The soldiers concentrated their fire on the people in the pits, and we fought back as well as we could with guns and bows, but we had only a few guns. The troops did not rush in and fight hand to hand, but once or twice after they had killed many of the men in a certain pit, they rushed in and finished up the work, killing the wounded and the women and children that had not been hurt. The fight here was kept up until nearly sundown, when at last the commanding officer called off his men and all started back down the creek toward the camp that they had driven us from. As they went back, the soldiers scalped the dead lying in the bed of the stream and cut up the bodies in a manner that no Indian could equal. Little Bear told me recently that after the fight he saw the soldiers scalping the dead and saw an old woman who had been scalped by the soldiers walk about, but unable to see where to go. Her whole scalp had been taken and the skin of her forehead fell down over her eyes.

At the beginning of the attack Black Kettle, with his wife and White Antelope,[3] took their position before Black Kettle's lodge and remained there after all others had left the camp. At last Black Kettle, seeing that it was useless to stay longer, started to run, calling out to White Antelope to follow him, but White Antelope refused and stood there ready to die, with arms folded, singing his death song—"Nothing lives long, except the earth and the mountains"—until he was shot down by the soldiers.

---

[2] Chivington's men—the soldiers under Colonel John Chivington, the military commander of the Colorado Territory.

[3] White Antelope—another chief of the Cheyenne people and a close friend of Black Kettle.

Black Kettle and his wife followed the Indians in their flight up the dry bed of the creek. The soldiers pursued them, firing at them constantly, and before the two had gone far, the woman was shot down. Black Kettle supposed she was dead and, the soldiers being close behind him, continued his flight. The troops followed him all the way to the rifle pits, but he reached them unhurt. After the light he returned down the stream looking for his wife's body. Presently he found her alive and not dangerously wounded. She told him that after she had fallen wounded, the soldiers had ridden up and again shot her several times as she lay there on the sand. Black Kettle put her on his back and carried her up the stream until he met a mounted man, and the two put her on the horse. She was taken to the Cheyenne camp on Smoky Hill. When she reached there, it was found that she had nine wounds on her body. My brother Charlie was in the camp, and he and Jack Smith, another half blood,[4] were captured. After the fight the soldiers took Jack Smith out and shot him in cold blood. Some of the officers told Colonel Chivington what the men were about and begged him to save the young man, but he replied curtly that he had given orders to take no prisoners and that he had no further orders to give. Some of the soldiers shot Jack and were going to shoot my brother also, but fortunately among the troops there were a number of New Mexican scouts whom Charlie knew, and these young fellows protected him. A few of our women and children were captured by the soldiers, but were turned over to my father at the fort, with the exception of two little girls and a boy, who were taken to Denver and there exhibited as great curiosities.

Soon after the troops left us, we came out of the pits and began to move slowly up the stream. More than half of us were wounded and all were on foot. When we had

---

[4] half blood—person of mixed Indian and white parentage.

gone up the stream a few miles, we began to meet some of our men who had left camp at the beginning of the attack and tried to save the horses which were being driven off by the soldiers. None of these men had more than one rope, so each one could catch only a single horse. As they joined us, the wounded were put on these ponies' backs. Among these men was my cousin, a young Cheyenne, from whom I secured a pony. I was so badly wounded that I could hardly walk.

When our party had gone about ten miles above the captured camp, we went into a ravine and stopped there for the night. It was very dark and bitterly cold. Very few of us had warm clothing, for we had been driven out of our beds and had had no time to dress. The wounded suffered greatly. There was no wood to be had, but the unwounded men and women collected grass and made fires. The wounded were placed near the fires and covered with grass to keep them from freezing. All night long the people kept up a constant **hallooing**[5] to attract the attention of any Indians who might be wandering about in the sand hills. Our people had been scattered all over the country by the troops, and no one knows how many of them may have been frozen to death in the open country that night.

We left this comfortless ravine before day and started east toward a Cheyenne camp on the Smoky Hill, forty or fifty miles away. The wounded were all very stiff and sore, and could hardly mount. My hip was swollen with the cold, and I had to walk a long way before I could mount my horse. Not only were half our party wounded, but we were obliged also to look out for a large number of women and little children. In fact, it was on the women and children that the brunt of this terrible business fell. Over three-fourths of the people killed in the battle were women and children.

---

[5] **hallooing**—shouting loudly with the intent of attracting attention.

We had not gone far on our way before we began to meet Indians from the camp on the Smoky Hill. They were coming, bringing us horses, blankets, cooked meat, and other supplies. A few of our people had succeeded in getting horses when the soldiers began the attack, and these men had ridden to the Smoky Hill River and sent aid back to us from the camp there. Almost everyone in that camp had friends or relatives in our camp, and when we came in sight of the lodges,[6] everyone left the camp and came out to meet us, wailing and mourning in a manner that I have never heard equaled.

A year after this attack on our camp a number of investigations of the occurrence were made. Colonel Chivington's friends were then extremely anxious to prove that our camp was hostile, but they had no facts in support of their statements. It was only when these investigations were ordered that they began to consider the question; at the time of the attack it was of no interest to them whether we were hostiles or friendlies. One of Chivington's most trusted officers recently said: "When we came upon the camp on Sand Creek we did not care whether these particular Indians were friendly or not." It was well known to everybody in Denver that the Colonel's orders to his troops were to kill Indians, to "kill all, little and big."

---

[6] lodges—dome-shaped dwellings made with log frames and covered with earth, common among the Indians of the upper Great Plains.

QUESTIONS TO CONSIDER

1. What did Black Kettle and White Antelope do when the soldiers first attacked? How did each one react when the firing continued?

2. What impression do you get of the Cheyenne people from Brent's account?

History of Nez Percé

BY JAMES REUBEN (NEZ PERCÉ)

The Nez Percé Indians originally inhabited southern Oregon, but were forced by the United States government onto a reservation in Idaho. After disagreements with white authorities in 1877, Chief Joseph (called "Young Joseph" in the following poem) decided to seek freedom for his people in Canada. At the head of a group that included many women and children, Joseph skillfully fought and outmaneuvered more than 2,000 United States soldiers for four months as he struggled to reach the Canadian border. Joseph and the Nez Percé people were finally captured only forty miles short of their destination and taken to an Oklahoma reservation. In 1880, a Nez Percé man named James Reuben wrote the following poem telling of the sufferings that war, disease, and white injustice had brought to his people. Reuben placed his poem beneath the cornerstone of a school built on the Nez Percé reservation, where it was found many years later and finally published in 1934.

They lived and enjoyed the happiness and freedom
and lived just as happy as any other Nation in the World.

But alas the day was coming when all their happy days
was to be turned into day of sorrow and moaning.

Their days of freedom was turned to be the day of slavery.

Their days of victory was turned to be conquered,
and their rights to the country was disregarded by
     another nations
which is called "Whiteman" at present day.

In 1855 a treaty was made between Nez Percé Nation
     and United States.

Wal-la-mot-kin (Hair tied on forehead) or Old Joseph,[1]
Hul-lal-ho-sot or (Lawyer),[2]
were the two leading Chiefs of the Nez Percé Nation in
     1855,
both of these two Chiefs consented to the treaty
and Nez Percé sold to the United States
part of their country.

In 1863 another treaty was made
in which Lawyer and his people consented
but Joseph and his people refused to make the second
     treaty

From that time Joseph's people
were called None-treaty Nez Percé.

---

[1] Old Joseph—Young Joseph's father.

[2] Lawyer—Nez Percé chief who agreed to an 1863 treaty that reduced the
Nez Percé reservation in Idaho from 10,000 to 1,000 square miles.

The treaty Nez Percé number 1,800

None-treaty numbered 1,000

The Nez Percé decreased greatly since 1805 up to 1863.
The smallpox prevailed among the tribe
which almost destroyed the tribe.

Lawyer's people advanced in civilization
    and became farmers etc.
They had their children in schools.

While Joseph's people refused all these things
they lived outside what was called Nez Percé Reservation

1877 Government undertook to move Young Joseph
    people on the Res.[3]

At this date Young Joseph was the ruling chief
son of Old Chief Joseph who died in 1868,
and left his people in charge of his own Son

Joseph and his followers broke out
and there was Nez Percé War bloody one
nine great battles fought

the last battle lasted five days
which Joseph surrendered with his people

1,000 Indians had went on the war path
but when Joseph surrendered
there was only 600

---

[3] Res—reservation.

400 killed during the wars
or went to other tribes.

after the capture Joseph was brought to this Territory as
  captives.

at present Joseph people numbers 350 out of 600
all are suffering on account of this Southern climate
result is he and his people
will live and die in this country exiled from home

Take it in the right light—
Nez Percé have been wrongly treated by the Government
it cannot be denied
not Nez Percé only but all other Indian Nations in
  America.

I wrote this about my own people.

I am a member of Nez Percé Tribe
and Nephew of Chief Joseph.

When this is opened and read [it] may be understood
how the Indians have been treated by the Whiteman.

QUESTIONS TO CONSIDER

1. How did the opinions of the Nez Percé leaders change
   between the time of the treaties of 1855 and 1863?

2. What happened to the people of Young Joseph after the
   Nez Percé War?

3. Why, in your opinion, did James Reuben write this poem?

from

A Short History of the Indians of the U.S.

BY FRANCIS LA FLESCHE (OMAHA)

*Once the Indians were contained on reservations, the United States
government and many Christian organizations sought to convert
them to the white man's way of life. This meant that young Native
Americans were to give up their traditional culture, religious beliefs,
language, dress—even their names. Schools were established to
educate this first generation of newly reoriented Indians. The author
of this selection, Francis La Flesche, was an Omaha Indian who
attended such a school. He went on to become a noted teacher and
writer, while one of his sisters was the first Indian woman to become
a medical doctor. Looking back on his school experience many
years later, La Flesche describes the strengths of his native Indian
language and culture as well as the misunderstandings of his often
poorly educated white teachers, who assumed they were improving
the children of an inferior civilization. This excerpt, written in 1900,
is from the preface to La Flesche's book about his schoolboy years,*
A Short History of the Indians of the U. S.

Among my earliest recollections are the instructions wherein we were taught respect and courtesy toward our elders; to say "thank you" when receiving a gift, or when returning a borrowed article; to use the proper and conventional term of relationship when speaking to another; and never to address any one by his personal name; we were also forbidden to pass in front of persons sitting in the tent without first asking permission; and we were strictly enjoined never to stare at visitors, particularly at strangers. To us there seemed to be no end to the things we were obliged to do, and to the things we were to refrain from doing.

From the earliest years the Omaha[1] child was trained in the grammatical use of his native tongue. No slip was allowed to pass uncorrected, and as a result there was no child-talk[2] such as obtains among English-speaking children—the only difference between the speech of old and young was in the pronunciation of words which the infant often failed to utter correctly, but this difficulty was soon overcome, and a boy of ten or twelve was apt to speak as good Omaha as a man of mature years.

Like the grown folk, we youngsters were fond of companionship and of talking. In making our gamesticks[3] and in our play, we chattered incessantly of the things that occupied our minds, and we thought it a hardship when we were obliged to speak in low tones while older people were engaged in conversation. When we entered the Mission School,[4] we experienced a greater hardship, for there we encountered a rule that prohibited the use of our own language, which rule was rigidly enforced with a hickory rod, so that the newcomer, however

---

[1] Omaha—a Native American people who originally occupied territory in what is now Nebraska.

[2] child-talk—baby talk.

[3] gamesticks—sticks used in Native American games such as lacrosse.

[4] Mission School—one of many schools established by Christian churches to educate Indian children in white American culture and the Christian religion.

socially inclined, was obliged to go about like a little dummy until he had learned to express himself in English.

All the boys in our school were given English names, because their Indian names were difficult for the teachers to pronounce. Besides, the **aboriginal**[5] names were considered by the missionaries as **heathenish**,[6] and therefore should be **obliterated**.[7] No less heathenish in their origin were the English substitutes, but the loss of their original meaning and significance through long usage had rendered them fit to continue as **appellations**[8] for civilized folk. And so, in the place of Tae-noo'-ga-wa-zhe, came Philip Sheridan;[9] in that of Wa-pah'-dae, Ulysses S. Grant,[10] that of Koo'-we-he-ge-ra, Alexander, and so on. Our sponsors went even further back in history, and thus we had our David and Jonathan, Gideon and Isaac, and, with the flood of these new names, came Noah.[11] It made little difference to us that we had to learn the significance of one more word as applied to ourselves, when the task before us was to make our way through an entire strange language. So we learned to call each other by our English names, and continued to do so even after we left school and had grown to manhood.

The names thus acquired by the boys are used in these sketches in preference to their own, for the reason that Indian words are not only difficult to pronounce, but are apt to sound all alike to one not familiar with the language and the boys who figure in these pages might

---

[5] **aboriginal**—relating to the earliest known population of a region, here Indian.

[6] **heathenish**—not belonging to Christians, thus, to the missionaries, uncivilized and unacceptable.

[7] **obliterated**—removed from memory.

[8] **appellations**—names.

[9] Philip Sheridan—Union general in the American Civil War (1861–65) who later led troops against the Indians of the Great Plains. Sheridan was regarded as a hero by those who were bestowing names on the Indian children.

[10] Ulysses S. Grant—commander of the Union forces in the American Civil War and later president of the United States (1869–77).

[11] David, Jonathan, Gideon, Isaac, . . . Noah—names from the Old Testament of the Christian Bible.

lose their identity and fail to stand out clearly in the mind of the reader were he obliged to continually struggle with their Omaha names.

In the talk of the boys I have striven to give a reproduction of the peculiar English spoken by them, which was **composite**,[12] gathered from the **imperfect comprehension**[13] of their books, the **provincialisms**[14] of the teachers, and the slang and bad grammar picked up from uneducated white persons employed at the school or at the Government Agency.[15] Oddities of speech, profanity, localisms, and slang were unknown in the Omaha language, so when such expressions fell upon the ears of these lads they innocently learned and used them without the slightest suspicion that there could be bad as well as good English.

This **misconception**[16] of Indian life and character common among the white people has been largely due to an ignorance of the Indian's language, of his mode of thought, his beliefs, his ideals, and his native institutions. Every aspect of the Indian and his manner of life have always been strange to the white man, and this strangeness has been magnified by the mists of prejudice and the conflict of interests between the two races. While these in time may disappear, no Native American can ever cease to regret that the utterances of his father have been constantly belittled when put into English, that their thoughts have frequently been **travestied**[17] and their native dignity obscured. The average interpreter has generally picked up his knowledge of English in a random fashion, for very few have ever had the advantage of a thorough education,

---

[12] **composite**—made up of different parts.

[13] **imperfect comprehension**—poor understanding.

[14] **provincialisms**—words or expressions associated with or used in a specific geographic area that are not considered standard English.

[15] Government Agency—any office of the Bureau of Indian Affairs that supervised Native American reservations.

[16] **misconception**—incorrect or inaccurate understanding.

[17] **travestied**—exaggerated in a grotesque or debased way.

and all have had to deal with the difficulties that attend the translator. The beauty and **picturesqueness**,[18] and **euphonious**[19] playfulness, or the **gravity of diction**[20] which I have heard among my own people, and other tribes as well, are all but impossible to be given literally in English.

The talk of the older people, when they speak in this book, is, as well as I can translate it, that of every day use.

Most of the country now known as the state of Nebraska (the Omaha name of the river Platt, descriptive of its shallowness, width, and low banks) had for many generations been held and claimed by our people as their own, but when they **ceded**[21] the greater part of this territory to the United States government, they reserved only a certain tract for their own use and home. It is upon the eastern part of this reservation that the scene of these sketches is laid, and at the time when the Omahas were living near the Missouri River in three villages, some four or five miles apart. The one farthest south was known as Ton'-won-ga-hae's village; the people were called "wood eaters," because they cut and sold wood to the settlers who lived near them. The middle one was Ish'-ka-da-be's village, and the people designated as "those who dwell in earth lodges," they having **adhered**[22] to the aboriginal form of dwelling when they built their village. The one to the north and nearest the Mission was E-sta'-ma-za's village, and the people were known as the "make-believe white-men," because they built their houses after the fashion of the white settlers. Furniture, such as beds, chairs, tables, bureaus, etc., were not used in any of these villages, except in a few instances, while in all of them the Indian costume, language, and social customs remained as yet **unmodified**.[23]

---

[18] **picturesqueness**—unusual attractiveness.

[19] **euphonious**—pleasant sounding; melodic.

[20] **gravity of diction**—seriousness in formal speech.

[21] **ceded**—surrendered or given up by treaty.

[22] **adhered**—remained attached.

[23] **unmodified**—unchanged.

In those days the Missouri was the only highway of commerce. Toiling slowly against the swift current, **laden**[24] with supplies for the trading posts and for our Mission, came the puffing little steamboats from the "town of the Red-hair," as St. Louis was called by the Indians, in memory of the auburn locks of Governor [William] Clark—of Lewis and Clark fame. We children used to watch these noisy boats as they forced their way through the **turbid**[25] water and made a landing by running the bow into the soft bank.

The white people speak of the country at this period as "a wilderness," as though it was an empty tract without human interest or history. To us Indians it was as clearly defined then as it is today; we knew the boundaries of tribal lands, those of our friends and those of our foes; we were familiar with every stream, the contour of every hill, and each peculiar feature of the landscape had its tradition. It was our home, the scene of our history, and we loved it as our country.

---

[24] **laden**—weighed down with a heavy load.

[25] **turbid**—muddy or unclear.

QUESTIONS TO CONSIDER

1. How does the author explain the reasons for changing the names of his fellow students and the language they spoke?

2. What differences did the author notice in the way that the Omaha people spoke their language compared to the way the whites spoke English?

3. What does the author say were the limitations of the Indian interpreters when they explained what the Indians were saying to white people?

4. How do you suppose the interpreters' limitations affected the way that white people regarded the Indians?

The Hopi Push
of War

BY HELEN SEKAQUAPTEWA (HOPI)

The question of whether to attend white-run Indian schools and accept white ways brought strong differences of opinion to the surface on some reservations. In 1906, the Hopi people of the Oraibi Pueblo in Arizona were bitterly divided. The "Friendlies" thought it best to accept the demands of white authorities, while the "Hostiles" wanted to resist what they saw as a serious threat to their identity as a people. Helen Sekaquaptewa, a village resident, describes the way in which her people settled the issue: Avoiding serious violence, the two sides engaged in a "pushing contest." She introduces her historical account in traditional Indian form by explaining the events in her narrative as the fulfillment of a prophecy. Her narrative expresses the frustration and sadness felt by her people as they confronted the dividing line that "assimilation"—the acceptance of white ways—created within their community.

Frequently **reiterated**[1] during this time was a prophecy that there would come a time when the village

---

[1] **reiterated**—repeated or retold.

would be divided and one of the groups would be driven off the **mesa**[2] forever and that the decision of who should go and who should stay was to hinge upon the ability of one party to push the other over a line which should be drawn on the ground.

The crisis was **precipitated**[3] prematurely during the first week of September, 1906, when the two factions came to an actual physical struggle. Tewaquaptewa,[4] whose following was slightly outnumbered by the Hostiles, received private information of a plot to assassinate him; indeed he understood that the Shungopovis,[5] rather than the Oraibians, were the **instigators**[6] of the plot. Tewaquaptewa called his council together that night at his house on the northern edge of the village, September 6, and they spent the night preparing for an attack on the Hostiles in the morning. During the night he sent word to Yokeoma[7] and his followers, who were also in council, that the Shungopovis would have to leave at once and that anyone taking their part must leave with them. . . .

Thereupon, the Friendlies set about clearing the village of Shungopovis. They began at the very spot where they stood; but every Friendly who laid hold of a Shungopovi to put him out of doors was attacked from behind by an Oraibi Hostile, so that the three went wrestling and struggling out of the door together. There was great commotion as the Friendlies carried out the Hostiles, pushing and pulling, the Hostiles resisting, struggling, kicking, and pulling the hair of their adversaries. The Hostiles were taken bodily, one by one to the northern outskirts of the village, and put down on

---

[2] **mesa**—large hill with a flat top and deeply sloping sides.

[3] **precipitated**—abruptly brought about.

[4] Tewaquaptewa—leader of the Friendlies (those friendly to whites).

[5] Shungopovis—members of a nearby village who may have had a grudge against Tewaquaptewa.

[6] **instigators**—those who stir up; the urgers or prodders.

[7] Yokeoma—priest who led the Hostiles (those hostile to "American" ways).

the far side of a line which had been scratched in the sandstone, parallel to the village, some time before.

After evicting the Hostile men, the Friendlies went into each home and forcibly ejected each family, driving them out to join their menfolk on the other side of The Line. A struggling stream of humanity—men, women, and children—poured out of their houses past Tewaquaptewa's house and out of the village, being shoved and dragged and pulled by Tewaquaptewa and his excited followers. Those resisting had their clothing torn and were bruised and scratched; the majority went passively, carrying burdens, the men with set faces and the women and children frightened and crying. . . .

My father, knowing that trouble was brewing, had told the boy who took his sheep out that day to drive them toward the Hotevilla spring that night. He spent the night in the Hostile council. My mother, hearing the rumor that we might be expelled from the village, had made ready some food, a jug of water, and blankets.

There was an underground little room in our house, our secret hiding place in case of war or trouble. The entrance was a hole in the floor, covered with a sheepskin on which my mother sat as she ground her corn. There was a little window to the outside for light and air. On this morning mother put her children into this hiding place—my married sister, Verlie, about sixteen; my brother Rincon, twelve; myself, seven; and my brother Henry, two. She watched and kept telling us what was happening, saying, "Don't be afraid. Nothing will happen to you." After a while she lifted the sheepskin and said for us to come on out. She started helping us up, as the sides were steep. Just at that moment, in came Tewaquaptewa's men, who started jerking us out. I was so little, I can't remember it all. One of the men said, "The time has come for you to go, so come on out of your hiding place. . . ."

We walked into the **plaza**[8] and were driven out of the village with the others. Many of the Friendly women sat on the flat housetops clapping their hands and yelling at us, making fun of us as we walked away from our home and village. . . .

Around four o'clock Yokeoma finally yielded to the continued pressure from the Friendlies. He stood up, and with all eyes on him, took a sharp rock in his hand and drew a line on the sandrock. Taking his stand with his back to the line he said, "Well, it will have to be this way now. If you pass me over this line, then I will walk." (He meant that he and his people would leave.)

Tewaquaptewa immediately jumped to the challenge. The two chiefs faced each other, each with his hands on the shoulders of his opponent. Their men rushed into the conflict, each eager to add his weight and exert his strength. Yokeoma was tall and thin. He was pushed up above the heads of the mass, gasping for breath; then he disappeared, and eventually he was passed over the line. A shout went up as Yokeoma, badly **disheveled**[9] and trampled, was helped to his feet, and his men made sure that he was not hurt. As soon as he could collect himself, Yokeoma left the knot of men around him and started walking the trail to the Hotevilla spring. We all gathered our bundles and followed him.

It was dark when we got to the spring, but soon there were forty or fifty campfires burning, and preparations for sleeping under the trees were under way. A few days later it rained, and the weather turned colder. A shelter of brush and trees was thrown up, reinforced with blankets, shawls, **gunny sacks**,[10] and pieces of old canvas, anything for protection against the cold. The dreary picture of the women and children crouching

---

[8] **plaza**—open area in the center of the village.

[9] **disheveled**—untidy and disarranged.

[10] **gunny sacks**—sacks made of coarse material such as burlap.

under this crude shelter persuaded Tewaquaptewa to further **leniency**.[11] He gave four more days in which the Hostiles might go into the village, in groups of three, and bring out their belongings. Many Hostiles expressed themselves: "We don't want to go back to the village and get our food. We want to go back to our homes and live there as we have always done."

Superintendent Lemmon[12] said to Yokeoma, "I am sorry that you are going away. I want you here for my friend." Yokeoma replied, "I do not want to go away from here." And the misery in the old man's face testified that the words came from his heart. . . .

It had been understood that the Mesa Verde area in Colorado was to be our destination. Some of the **clans**[13] claimed to have originated there. But after about a week, Yokeoma stood by the spring one morning, looked out over the valley, and said, "I am staying here. Anyone who wants to, can go on." None were anxious, and none did go on.

There are many big flat sandstones cropping out of the ground on the outskirts of Old Oraibi. One of them marks The Line. An inscription was scratched there by a young man named Robert Selena. Robert was a student at the Indian School at Keams Canyon and was home in the summer of 1906. He took it upon himself to mark the spot:

WELL IT HAVE TO BE DONE
THIS WAY NOW
THAT WHEN YOU PASS ME OVER THIS LINE
IT WILL BE DONE
SEPT. 8, 1906

---

[11] **leniency**—mercy.

[12] Superintendent Lemmon—white official who supervised the reservation for the United States Bureau of Indian Affairs.

[13] **clans**—groups within a Native American tribe who trace their lineage back to a common ancestor.

QUESTIONS TO CONSIDER

1. What events and ideas led to the conflict in the Oraibi Pueblo?

2. What is your opinion of the way in which the conflict in the Oraibi Pueblo was settled?

3. What might have been the reasons Superintendent Lemmon was sorry that Yokeoma and his people were leaving the village?

4. What is your interpretation of the sandstone inscription made by Robert Selena and printed at the end of the story?

We Missed the Bus

BY GEORGE PEEQUAQUAT

(SAULTEAUX-OJIBWAY)

The United States government's attempts to reform Indian policy often had little effect on the day-to-day life of the poorest people on the reservation. The following story took place in southern Canada in the late 1940s, when conditions and practices were very similar to those in the United States. The narrator, George Peequaquat, is a member of the Saulteaux-Ojibway tribe. This tragic memory from his childhood illustrates the deep misunderstanding that existed between people of Indian and non-Indian cultures and the consequences that his well-meaning father suffered as a result.

I was five years old when I first attended the Lestock Indian Residential School[1] in 1948. Lestock is 100 miles from Nut Lake.[2] In those days it seemed like a thousand miles. From home our parents took us to the farm instructor's office where the Residence truck was waiting.

---

[1] Lestock Indian Residential School—boarding school for Indian children in the Canadian province of Saskatchewan. The school was operated from 1898 to 1976 by Roman Catholic missionaries.

[2] Nut Lake—Ojibwa (Chippewa) Indian reserve in Saskatchewan, Canada.

No matter how cold it was we traveled in the back of the truck. It had a **tarpaulin**[3] over the top. In the winter we used it for hockey trips. When it got really cold we made a wood fire in the little stove in one corner of the truck box. Temperatures sometimes dipped to minus forty.

But when we went to school in the fall we didn't need the stove. The size of the group increased as we went from reserve[4] to reserve. It was not uncommon to have up to forty children ranging in age from five to sixteen piled in the back of the truck.

Every autumn the truck would come to collect children from the reserves in our area. The farm instructor was notified of the date that the truck was going to arrive. He then notified all the parents of school-age children.

Parents often sent their children to residential school because they were assured that there was plenty of food at the school. They knew that their children would not starve over the winter. Starvation was a very real scare. If the hunting and gathering had not been good or the store of food was not adequate to get us through the winter, we starved. This was in the late 1940s when the rest of the country was experiencing the post-war boom.[5] Often one less mouth to feed made the difference in being able to last the winter. Sending the children to residential school solved part of the food problem, but it did nothing to keep our families together. I remember the hurt in my parents' faces when they couldn't provide enough food and had to send us away.

Most of the parents could not read and did not understand about calendars. If they missed the date that their children were to be picked up, they were thrown in jail.

One time my dad got his weeks mixed up and missed the truck, so we went back home. A few days

---

[3] **tarpaulin**—sheet of waterproof canvas.

[4] reserve—lands set aside for Indians are called "reserves" in Canada and "reservations" in the United States.

[5] post-war boom—the economic prosperity that followed World War II.

later, two policemen and the priest from Lestock came to the camp where we were living. People were **transient**[6] in those days and we lived in camps. There were no permanent houses or settlements on the reserve. Our home was a big white tent. Some of our people still lived in teepees. So-May, one of the elders, and other old people preferred the teepee. When the priest and policemen came to our camp, the priest took us school children along with him to school. I think his name was Father Belladeaux. We didn't know the difference between the priests. They all looked the same. He was driving a dark panel truck.

The policemen took my father off to jail.

We didn't have holidays till the following June. There were no open weekends or breaks when we were allowed to go home for a visit during the year—not even at Christmas time.

When we got back from school in June, Dad was back at home. We never found out how long he had spent in jail. He never understood why he was sent to jail.

---

[6] **transient**—moving from place to place.

QUESTIONS TO CONSIDER

1. What were the conditions that led the parents in Lestock to send their children to the Indian boarding school?

2. What cultural differences were responsible for the tragedy in this story?

3. What effect did the school have on the families of the students?

4. In your opinion, why didn't the author's father understand the reason he was put in jail?

DIAN LAND FOR SALE

A HOME

OF

UR OWN

❋

PAYMENTS

Destruction

PERFECT TITLE

❋

POSSESSION

WITHIN

THIRTY DAYS

NE LANDS IN THE WEST

RIGATED
RIGABLE

GRAZING

AGRICULTURAL
DRY FARMING

HE DEPARTMENT OF THE INTERIOR SOLD UNDER SEALED BIDS ALLOTTED INDIAN LAND AS FOLLOWS:

ocation.	Acres.	Average Price per Acre.	Location.	Acres.	Average Price per Acre.
	5,211.21	$7.27	Oklahoma	34,664.00	$19.14
	17,013.00	24.85	Oregon	1,020.00	15.43
	1,684.50	33.45	South Dakota	120,445.00	16.53
	11,034.00	9.86	Washington	4,879.00	41.37
a	5,641.00	36.65	Wisconsin	1,069.00	17.00
akota	22,610.70	9.93	Wyoming	865.00	20.64

YEAR 1911 IT IS ESTIMATED THAT 350,000 ACRES WILL BE OFFERED FOR SALE

In 1911, the Department of the Interior offered "surplus" land for sale. The land
was taken from Native American tribes when they were forced onto reservations.

After the Great Sioux Uprising was put down, soldiers and townspeople gathered to witness the executions of thirty-eight Sioux Indians in Mankato, Minnesota, on December 26, 1862. See page 86. ▶

United States Army cavalry officers pursue Native Americans in 1876. Often even small bands of rebels were tracked down by the cavalry and sent to reservations, discouraging others from revolting.
▼

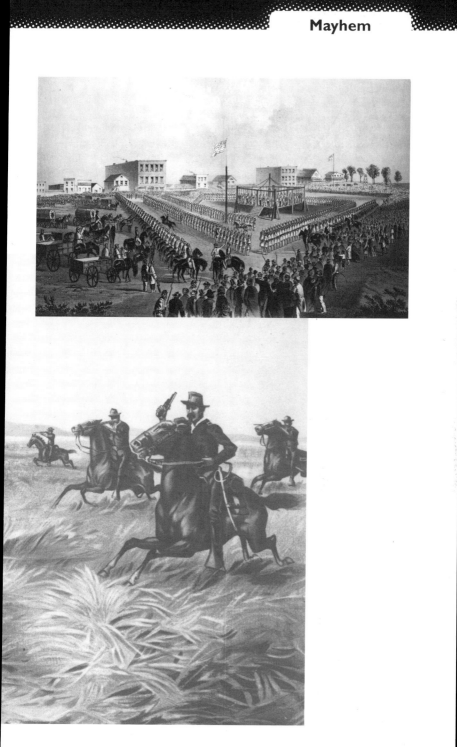

One way in which the federal government attempted to assimilate Native Americans into white culture was to send Native children away to boarding schools. The Carlisle Indian School in Pennsylvania was one such school. A group of Chiricahua Apaches from southern Arizona were sent to Carlisle in the 1880s to learn useful trades.

A.

PRIMER
FOR THE

USE of the MOHAWK CHILDREN,
To acquire the Spelling and Reading
of their own: As well as to get acquainted with the English Tongue,
which for that purpose is put on the
opposite Page.

WAERIGHWAGHSAWE IKSA-
ONGOENWA Tsiwaondad-derigh-
honny Kaghyadoghsera; Nayondewe-
yestaghk ayeweanaghnodon ayeghyì-
dow Kaniyenkehàga Kaweanondaghk-
kouh; Dyorheaf-hàga oni tsinihadiwea-
notea.

Montreal, Printed at Fleury Mesplet,
1781.

Mohawk primer. ▶

Apache students on
first arriving.
▼

▲
Native American girls learning home economics the white way.

Apache boys after four months.
▼

One of the most famous Native American rebellions was led by Crazy Horse, an Oglala Sioux warrior and later chief, who led the fight in the Sioux Wars of the 1860s and 1870s. On June 25, 1876, Crazy Horse led his troops into battle at Little Bighorn in Montana, where his forces crushed cavalry led by General George Armstrong Custer. After a relentless pursuit by army troops, Crazy Horse surrendered. On September 5, 1877, he died after being bayoneted by a soldier at Fort Robinson, Nebraska.

▲

"Our first impulse was to escape with our squaws and papooses [babies], but we were so hemmed in that we had to fight."

▲
Sioux war.

▲
Mourning the dead.

In 1831, the Cherokee Nation sued the state of Georgia in a case that reached the Supreme Court. Chief Justice John Marshall delivered the opinion of the court, which stated that Georgia could forcibly remove the Cherokees. During the brutal winter of 1838–39, the Cherokees were removed from Georgia and forced to walk to what is now Oklahoma. Known as the "Trail of Tears," this journey resulted in the deaths of 4,000 Cherokees. Ironically, the Cherokee were one of the most assimilated groups, with a written language created by Sequoyah in 1821.

▲
Sequoyah.

Cherokee *Phoenix* newspaper.

▼

Trail of Tears.

Survival

Evaluating the Indian Reorganization Act

BY ALFRED DUBRAY (HO-CHUNK)
AND RAMON ROUBIDEAUX (SIOUX)

When he took office in 1933, President Franklin D. Roosevelt promised a "New Deal" for the American people, and, as part of his program, he appointed John Collier to be commissioner of the Bureau of Indian Affairs. Collier was an idealist who proposed the Indian Reorganization Act (IRA), which brought about a dramatic change in the government's Indian policy for the first time in half a century. Under the IRA, Indian tribes were to be encouraged to establish their own councils, to increase the size of their reservations, and to restore their social and cultural traditions. As the two interviews from the 1960s indicate, Native Americans held different opinions of the IRA. Alfred DuBray, a Ho-Chunk leader who became superintendent of the Winnebago reservation in 1970, speaks approvingly of the changes that the IRA brought to his reservation. However, Ramon Roubideaux, a Lakota Sioux and well-known South Dakota attorney, saw the IRA as little more than a new version of the same policies of white control over Indian life.

"It Had a Lot of Advantages"
by Alfred DuBray

I remember [when the Indian Reorganization Act was applied out at Rosebud, South Dakota.] I never had too much contact before with the agency.[1] We always lived way out in the country, and our contacts with the Bureau at that time were [with] what you would call farm agents, or boss farmers. These were abandoned districts in the outlying areas of the reservations. They would come around and keep us informed and deal with leases and things of this sort.

We lived in a community where there was quite a number of Indian families, many of whom were my relatives. They were quite politically minded—tribally, politically minded. I remember them talking about this New Deal[2] that was coming out at that time. Of course, this was in the administration of Franklin D. Roosevelt, and his new Commissioner, John Collier, who immediately proposed to Congress a new era for the American Indian people. He proposed to Congress this legislation.

This was a new deal for the Indians. Nobody really understood it. They knew that they were going to have to vote on whether they wanted it or not. Of course, it was very difficult many times to get things accurately to them. It was a matter of communication—very difficult because they would interpret in many ways the minor things. They had all kinds of stories going about the new program. Many were against, and many were for it. From what they understood of it, it was very difficult because it was such a radical change from their way of life. Really, their customs and practices up to that point—most of all their governing procedures in the

---

[1] agency—office of the United States Bureau of Indian Affairs on a reservation.

[2] New Deal—name given to President Franklin D. Roosevelt's social and economic policies designed to combat the effects of the Great Depression of the 1930s.

tribe—were handled through tribal leaders, designated by the chiefs, the leaders from one generation to another. They looked to the tribal chiefs, or leaders, to guide them in their procedures. They had no formal government of any kind, though they were fairly well organized.

Anyway, this was quite a radical change to bolt on. I think many of them looked at this as another way for government to take over more of their controls. But, finally, the Bureau got going on this and organized themselves fairly well, and established some positions as to the responsibilities of employees. They would go around to explain the Reorganization Act to the people on all the reservations as best they could. I remember the one on Rosebud—the reorganization man they called him—was Mr. Ben Reifel. He was a man who had been in Washington working for the Bureau and was very capable. He was selected as one of these men to go out in the Rosebud area and explain this—sell it, in other words. So he did. He spent quite a lot of time out there. Then, finally, they were given deadlines or dates to vote. I don't remember all the details on that, but I think they had a rather close vote, as I recall, on adopting the Reorganization Act on the Rosebud Reservation.

Of course, the point of interest was it had a lot of advantages, in that many of the people would have loan funds available—huge amounts. Farm programs were developed through this; cattle-ranging programs were initiated. Educational loans were beginning to be made available for the Indian youngsters who had never had any opportunity before to attend higher institutions. There was a new feeling there in education. And, of course, mainly the tribal governing body got busy there and established the governing body, voted on their representatives and their council meetings. It was, I think, difficult for the people to recognize what they were doing for probably several years, until they got into the change.

"A Paternalistic Type of Government"
by Ramon Roubideaux

As far as the Indian Reorganization Act is concerned, I think this is possibly one of the best intentioned but unfortunate happenings that could have possibly taken place as far as the Indian people are concerned. Although it did stop the sale of Indian lands and did stop the **allotment system**,[3] it created a **socialistic society**[4] and set the Indian people apart from the mainstream of American life and made them a problem. It has substituted in place of the governing system that the Indians had prior to the Indian Reorganization Act a white man's idea of how they should live—rather a **paternalistic**[5] type of government, which has as its object the socializing of all activities of the Indian people. While the framers of this act and the ones who are responsible for the idea of formulating it probably had the best intentions in the world, I cannot help but think that there was, maybe not an **overt**[6] conspiracy, but one on the back of the mind of these bureaucrats to really **perpetuate**[7] their own existence. . . .

To make myself a little clearer, I want to elaborate a little on the effects of the Indian Reorganization Act insofar as it has **deterred**[8] the development and the independent thinking of the Indian people. In the first place, it set the Indian aside as a problem. The Indian was told that he was a problem from the very day he was born under this system, and as he grew older, by the presence of these so-called experts in ranching and agriculture

---

[3] **allotment system**—a hated system that divided the land on Indian reservations and gave it to Indian families in 160-acre pieces. The remainder was then sold to the highest bidder, usually white.

[4] **socialistic society**—society in which the government owns all the property and land in the name of its citizens.

[5] **paternalistic**—like the relationship of a father toward his children whom he cares for because they can't care for themselves.

[6] **overt**—open and observable, not hidden or secret.

[7] **perpetuate**—cause to continue indefinitely; in this instance, to provide job security for the bureaucrats.

[8] **deterred**—prevented.

and other activities they were paying lip service[9] to teaching the Indians, he was somehow made to feel that he was inferior, that he wasn't able to compete. So that the whole system emphasized the activities of the Indians as a whole for the benefit of the whole, rather than the individual private enterprise system of our American system. He wasn't taught to be a capitalist, which he must be taught in order for him to survive in this country. . . .

And I think the main thing that was wrong with the whole thing was that the setting of the Indian aside on a different place in the state, designating him as a problem, making him feel he was a problem, beating down rebels, beating down Indians who expressed any independent thinking, rewarding **collaborators**,[10] rewarding them with positions of importance and completely stifling independent and creative thinking from the Indian people, having different laws apply to him, setting up a different kind of government. . . .

It's not self-government, because self-government by permission is no self-government at all. Everything that the Indian Reorganization Act brought in under the **guise**[11] of self-government was subject to the approval or the concurrence of the Secretary of the Interior or his authorized representative—the superintendent. These Indians have never made policy decisions; they have never been able to use creative thinking. Everything they've done has been under the wing of the government; it's just like the rich kid with the rich father. Everything is planned for him, he never develops this mind of his.

---

[9] paying lip service—agreeing without real conviction or action.

[10] **collaborators**—those who cooperate or work together with an enemy force occupying their territory.

[11] **guise**—pretense.

QUESTIONS TO CONSIDER

1. According to the two authors, why did the United States government pass the Indian Reorganization Act?

2. How do the two authors differ in their opinions on who benefited from the act?

3. Why does Alfred DuBray support the act?

4. What does Ramon Roubideaux mean when he says "self-government by permission is no self-government at all"?

5. In your opinion, which was the more persuasive argument? What is your opinion of the act?

Surviving
in the Cities

BY BELLE JEAN FRANCIS (ATHABASCAN)

AND BENNY BEARSKIN (WINNEBAGO)

In the middle of the twentieth century, the United States
government returned to policies that tried to assimilate—to absorb—
Indian people into mainstream American society. One such policy,
"relocation," encouraged select Native Americans to move from
the reservation into the unfamiliar territory of America's larger
cities. They were given financial help in moving to certain designated
cities and, for a brief period, helped to find housing and employment.
After that, the government had no further responsibility. Many
other Indians came to cities on their own, hoping for a better life.
Los Angeles, Denver, Minneapolis, Milwaukee, and Chicago were
among the cities that gained significant Indian populations. After
growing up on the reservation, most Indians needed far more
assistance, preparation, and psychological support than they were
given to adjust to urban life and its often unexpected challenges.
In the following selections, two Native Americans explain the
difficulties the new city dwellers faced and offer some insights in
managing the culture clash.

"A New Arrival, 1968"
by Belle Jean Francis

Here I am in a big city, right in the middle of Chicago. I don't know anybody. I am so lonesome and I have that urge to go home. I don't know which direction to go—south, north, east, or west. I can't just take any direction because I don't know my way around yet.

I see strange faces around me and I keep wondering how I will survive in this strange environment. I keep wondering how I can get over this loneliness, and start adjusting to this environment. I know I have to start somewhere along the line and get involved in social activities and overcome the fear I am holding inside me and replace it with courage, dignity, self-confidence, and the ambition to reach my goal.

Before I can adjust myself to this strange environment and get involved in things, I need friends who will help me overcome this urge to go home so I can accomplish my goal here in this unknown world which I [have] entered.

from Division Street: America
by Benny Bearskin (as interviewed by) Studs Terkel

Getting **urbanized**.[1] I like this term. It means you have to learn the ropes, just like a person moving out from the prairie country into the woods. You know, there are certain dangers in such a **transition**,[2] and it's the same way in a city. Yes, you have to learn the ropes. And once you become urbanized, this means to me that you're gonna settle down, and you have to have a goal to look forward to. Otherwise, I think it would drive you crazy.

---

[1] **urbanized**—citified; made into a city person.

[2] **transition**—passage from one state or place to another.

I came to Chicago in 1947, after I had been married, and later on I sent for my wife and my one child and since that time we've lived here in the city. The most important reason was that I could at least feel confident that [there would be] perhaps fifty paychecks a year here . . . and you can't always get that. Even though it might be more pleasant to be back home, for instance, [in] Nebraska.

What do you call home: Do you call Nebraska home?

Yes, I think this is one feature most Indians have in common. They have a deep attachment for the land. This has been so for a long, long time. Many different tribes of Indians are now residing in Chicago, but most of them maintain ties with the people back home. Even in cases where the older members of their families have passed away, they still make a point to go home. Many of them make the trip twice a year to go back to the place where they were born and raised. . . .

You put down on the application: INDIAN?

Yes, always. I think that's a source of pride. I think a lot of fellas think this is a source of pride, because we enjoy the distinction that no other person has. We are at home, while everyone else came here from somewhere else.

And I believe that, as time goes on, that society becomes more and more complex, there is that need for a basic pride in order to have something on which to build character. If you don't have that pride, well, then you have no identity. We understand that all the states have these mental institutions that are bulging at the seams. This is evidence of social and psychological **maladjustment.**[3] So we have to have some values, I believe. . . .

There are some areas where the transition from Indian culture to white culture is going on, and some of the children are born into a situation where the old values

---

[3] **maladjustment**—inability to adjust to the stresses of daily living.

are already lost. There being no basic economies in these areas, there's much poverty. And nothing of the white culture is available to them. So they're lost in between.

And it is this type of young Indian who is ashamed he is an Indian. Because he doesn't realize, there's nobody [who] ever told him: his ancestors were a noble race of men who developed over many centuries a way of life, primitive though it was; it existed without prisons, hospitals, jails, courts . . . , or insane asylums, or currency, or anything. Yet an Indian back in those days was able to live from babyhood till all the hair on his head became white, and he lived a life of complete fulfillment. With no regrets at the end. You rarely see that in this day and age.

Four of our children were born here in this city, and yet, I think, they're oriented as American Indians. I make it a point to take them on my vacation trips in the summer, always to a different reservation to get acquainted with the people of the tribe. We take photographs, we record the songs that are sung, we participate in dancing and compete for prizes. . . .

I think those Indians who retain the greatest amount of their cultural heritage are really very fortunate, because they feel that it's more important to retain one's dignity and integrity and go through life in this manner, than spending all their energy on an accumulation of material wealth. They find this a frustrating situation. I think the Indian is the only nationality under the system who has resisted this melting-pot concept.[4] Everybody else wants to jump in; they [Indians] view this idea, jumping in and becoming American, as losing identity.

I don't think the flame ever went out. Of course, we do have exceptions. We have many Indians who have been orphaned at an early age, who have

---

[4] melting-pot concept—idea that people in the United States should lose their ethnic identity and culture and become part of one standard American culture.

become completely **acculturated**[5] and know nothing of their heritage.

It's so impersonal. I think this makes itself felt in many situations. For instance, when you become urbanized, you learn how to think in abstract terms. Now when you get here on Broadway, to catch a CTA[6] bus going south, you subconsciously know there's a driver, but you take no interest in him at all as a person, he's more like an object. And it's the same way in schools. The teacher is there to do a certain function. And I think the teacher also feels that these pupils are like a bunch of bumps on a log. You know, this can be a difficult thing, especially for an Indian child, who, in his family life, learns to establish relationships on a person-to-person basis. And he finds that this is absent in the classroom. And frequently parents go to talk to the principal, to talk to the teacher; it's just like going over there talking to a brick wall. They feel you just aren't hip. Something is wrong with you, and if you don't conform, it's just too bad. . . .

Poverty is not merely the lack of wealth, a lack of money. It goes much deeper than that. There's poverty in reservations and where there are no reservations, and where there are no Indians. What we try to do here, at the Center [American Indian Center] is to some way, somehow, get people *involved*. Most of these people are coping with their problems on a day-to-day basis. The future is something that rarely enters their minds.

I think that perhaps my early training in the home impressed me with the philosophy of our forebears. It was taught to us that if one could be of service to his people, this is one of the greatest honors there is. I think this has been a strong influence on my life. I'll never know all the answers. I'm still learning the answers.

---

[5] **acculturated**—instilled in the culture of the mainstream society; Americanized.

[6] CTA—Chicago Transit Authority.

I think there will be some radical changes taking place. We have a younger generation, in the age bracket of my oldest daughter. I think in the future Indians will make a bigger contribution. It's been pointed out that Indians should feel that if it was not for the land which they owned, this would not be the greatest nation on earth. . . .

QUESTIONS TO CONSIDER

1. What are two things that Belle Jean Francis feels she must do in order to succeed in the city?

2. Why does Benny Bearskin feel that it is so important for Indian people to be proud of their heritage?

3. Why do you think that Benny Bearskin was able to make a successful adjustment to life in the city?

4. What do you think is his definition of poverty?

On an Indian Reservation: How Colonialism Works

BY ROBERT K. THOMAS (CHEROKEE)

The social movements of the 1960s brought major re-evaluations and changes to many areas of American society. Robert K. Thomas was one of a new generation of college-educated Native American activists who brought a fresh perspective to the study of Indian life on the reservation. Thomas felt that for a tribal culture to survive it needed to possess at least some of its original land, which, unlike the reservation, is often held to be spiritually sacred. He argued that tribes also need a unique religious system, the common use of their own language, and a sense of their own historical importance. In this essay, Thomas argues that the reservation system, often unintentionally, works against Indian interests and creates a system that he calls "internal colonialism." He relies on both his experience as a social scientist and his deep understanding of Indian societies to support his ideas.

An Indian reservation is the most complete colonial system[1] in the world that I know about. One of the things you find on Indian reservations is exploitation of natural resources. (Now, I don't want to give you the impression that the U.S. government goes out with big **imperialist**[2] designs on Indian reservations. Were it that simple, were there nice, clean-cut villains, you could just shoot them or something. But it isn't that simple.) Let us say that the U.S. government is in charge of the resources on an Indian reservation and cuts the timber. You have a "tribal sawmill," which is tribal only in the sense that it is located on the reservation, but people in the government bureaucracy actually run it. They're supposed to. They are legally told to do that and they have no choice. They aren't being "mean" to the Indians, they're just supposed to run the sawmill. If they don't run it, they lose their jobs, that's all.

So, the people who tend to get the jobs in the sawmill are the "responsible" Indians. Now, you can imagine who the responsible Indians are. They are people who are most like the whites in many ways, and hence the most "cooperative," that is, they keep their mouths shut and their noses clean. This makes for bitter **factionalism**[3] on many reservations, and is another outcome of this classic colonial structure. Accordingly, this kind of structure always creates an economic **elite**[4] of *marginal people*,[5] or cooperative marginal people. I don't want to give you the impression that all marginal people on all Indian reservations or in all countries around the world are economic elites, they aren't. (Sometimes, if they are marginal

---

[1] colonial system—economic system in which one country maintains control over another for the former's economic advantage.

[2] **imperialist**—like an empire controls its colonies.

[3] **factionalism**—state of conflict within an organization.

[4] **elite**—group or class enjoying superior status.

[5] *marginal people*—people on the edge of productive society, not in the mainstream.

enough, they become revolutionaries.) But this is one class of people created by the classic colonial structure.

When the resources are sold and the returns go into the tribal treasury, the people who have control of it, insofar as anybody on the Indian reservation has control of anything, are these marginal people. Their job is to **mediate**[6] between the Indian Bureau and the Indians, and they are the same people who work in the sawmill. They have very little power beyond that which the Bureau will give them. The raw materials from this reservation are, of course, sold outside of the reservation area. The U.S. government deducts from the sales of these resources the costs of providing social services to the reservation. (If any of you are familiar with the head-tax system in Africa and Asia,[7] for instance, you can see a very close resemblance.) The remaining money goes into the tribal treasury and, in turn, is allocated to further economic activity which is first planned and then **sanctioned**[8] by the government as before. What happens after a little while, what is bound to happen, is that the natural resources of this region are drained off. So, in a sense, you don't have economic change there at all.

What does an Indian experience in this situation? You have to make decisions in order to have experience, and few if any decisions here are taken by Indians.

Let's take another example: an industry that moves into an Indian reservation. I was on the Pine Ridge Indian reservation[9] when a fishhook plant was brought in. The Bureau administrators thought that this was good for the reservation because it would create jobs and bring in money. Buildings were built to lure in industry. After the buildings were finished and the industry

---

[6] **mediate**—resolve conflict.

[7] head-tax system in Africa and Asia—system of taxes European nations imposed on each person (head) in their colonies in Africa and Asia during the nineteenth and twentieth centuries.

[8] **sanctioned**—authorized or approved.

[9] Pine Ridge Indian reservation—Sioux reservation in South Dakota.

moved in, people were found to help recruit the labor for the industry. Because of the high transportation costs, the wages were not high, but, in the minds of the administrators, it was better than nothing—although many people referred to them as sweat shops.

So, they are now making fishhooks on the Pine Ridge reservation. Sioux males were recruited to provide the labor for the industry—to tie fishhooks. Do any of you know anything about the Sioux Indians? Well, they were the finest light cavalry the world has ever seen, the finest military organization, and the finest warriors in the world. They are also the most **thin-skinned**[10] men you've ever met—they'll hit you in the mouth at the drop of a hat. And they're supposed to tie feathers onto fishhooks? Not likely. So, right away it was defined as women's work—nice little ladies putting nice little feathers on nice little fishhooks. So, the Sioux men quit. This means they are faced with alternatives of being defined as irresponsible slobs by the people who are promoting industry, or as sissies by their own fellows—that's a big choice! You can either go in and tie those feathers to those fishhooks, while your buddies are out punching cattle—a man's job—or you can be an irresponsible slob, not providing for your families again.

And that is what happens in most colonial countries right across the world—the community lies **inert**[11] until prodded. That's what happens after a long history of not having experience, you are inert until prodded, i.e., nobody at the bottom or even among the **intermediaries**[12] acts until someone at the top acts in a way that you must respond.

And you are judged on how you respond. So, if a man from the top or intermediary group comes and asks

---

[10] **thin-skinned**—easily provoked; quick to take offense.

[11] **inert**—unable to move or take action.

[12] **intermediaries**—people who act as mediators or "go-betweens" with groups.

you whether or not you're going to work in a fishhook factory and you answer yes, then the rest of the community judges you on that reaction. They consider you a "white man's Indian," say. And after a certain amount of time people can only respond in terms of this structure and its movements, because all the institutions, information, and experience is located there.

Let's look at the cattle program. Every once in a while the U.S. decides it should sponsor an economic-agricultural activity. The government gives money to the people whose job it is to mediate between the government and the people. If you're on an Indian tribal council, you look to those people to tell you how to set up a program. How else could you do that? You've never seen a cattle program. You've never run one. You've never taken action very much yourself except in terms of waiting for these people to give you cues so you can act negatively or positively. Now you find out how to set up a cattle program. You set up a cattle program and you make individual loans. The intermediaries run the loan board, again because they are more like white men by virtue of their association with them—not because of their experience in making decisions for this community, but just because of their association with whites outside of the formal institutional context. So they run the loan board and then Sam Blackbird, say, comes in and wants to get a loan—a big strappin' Sioux Indian about thirty-two who's worked about two years since he was fifteen and the rest of the time he's lived with his folks. Well, you're not going to give money to Sam Blackbird. Suppose, for some unknown reason, Sam Blackbird would get a loan. Everybody would come over and say, "Gee, Sam, how lucky can you get—them guys up there finally gave you some money, so let's cut out one of these big steer here and eat it." Well, what is Sam going to do? He can act like a "lousy, greedy white man," which is what Indians think white men are—not be a Sioux, in other words—or he can **default**[13] on his loan. Those are the options that the structure offers him.

Now, in fact, what would happen is that Sam Blackbird would kill the steer and default on his loan. So, if you're going to start a cattle program in this community that isn't the way you would do it. But nobody in the community really knows that, because nobody has ever run a cattle program, and it's been so long since anybody ever did anything like a cattle program that there are really no **analogies**[14] to call on—they would just have to experiment around to find out how to run a cattle program, which they are not able to do. (As a social scientist,[15] I could just make a guess, it would be only a guess, that a group of brothers should be given financial responsibility and that might work. But, I don't know, it's been too long since this institution has functioned and decisions have been in their hands. Africa was never in this bad shape—the reservation is the most complete system of colonialism I know.)

Let me go back to the first point that I made about these two processes of change. What I've been talking about is really lack of change because the structure isolates the people from experience. Let me give you an example of how that could be different.

There was a small industry started by the University of Chicago among the Sac and Fox in Tama, Iowa. And it was a mess—everybody got mad right away. I remember I went out there one time and everybody had just walked off their jobs because somebody had said something to somebody (this is a kinship society, a tribe in which interpersonal relations are the most important thing). But they came back the next day because they also wanted the industry. In any case, all kinds of things changed at Tama—and really changed.

---

[13] **default**—fail to pay money when it is due.

[14] **analogies**—similar comparisons.

[15] social scientist—person who studies society and individual relationships in and to society.

Before the project, an Indian might work in Marshalltown, Iowa, say—and maybe an uncle would come over one day and say, "Joe, I want to go into town and buy some birthday gifts for my little niece, would you take me into town?" Joe has twenty minutes to go to work, but do you know what he does? He takes his uncle into town. He shows up the next day and the foreman says, "Where were you on Monday?" And he says, "I had to take my uncle into town." And the foreman says, "Holy mackerel, I've got a production deadline, and you have to take your uncle to town!" So he says, "Pick up your check, pal, you're through." And Joe's reaction is, "Well, those white people are mean, everybody knows that." So, he goes home. And then he has to wait another year before he ventures out to get another job.

Well, one of the things the Sac and Fox found out working in the project industry was that, if you went over and asked your nephew to take you into town at the time he was supposed to go up and work with the rest of his kinfolk, then all the other kinfolk got mad at you for asking him to do that. And that's the way that they learned about production deadlines. And they learned it. (Tribal people can be **coercive**.[16] They are not only friendly, smiling folk people. That's one side of them. They can also be as mean as hell, and can put controls on you like nobody's business.)

Here is another example. One of the Indians was in the process of drawing a sketch for a tile (the kind you put under hot things) when his uncle died. He was supposed to go into a four-day seclusion. It was two months before Christmas, with the Christmas rush coming up. Everybody wondered what they could do: "Charlie has to go into four-day seclusion. We're going to miss all this stuff for Christmas." So they went to their own priest. They sat around. Then he said, "Why don't you fix a

---

[16] **coercive**—forcibly controlling.

little place under the door so Charlie can make those designs and slip 'em out under the door. He doesn't have to touch anybody, or see anybody." And they worked that out so that Charlie could keep on working.

Now, that's experience and change. That's facing other kinds of people and your environment in terms of your own **aspirations**[17] and in terms of the kind of life you're leading.

Let me give you another example. In the early days of the project, they needed to organize industry, but these are tribal people, all relatives, and nobody likes to tell anybody else what to do. So, they got together and decided they're going to nominate someone for chairman because they've heard that whites do that sort of thing. So they nominate Dan, say, who almost crawls under the desk at the thought of having to tell his relatives what to do. So, then, everybody realizes maybe that isn't going to work so well, and they decide to abandon it. Finally, they figure out that the guy who had the most hours in the previous year would become chairman of the board in the industry. By the nature of the case, he didn't have to volunteer, the one with the most hours just had the job. Now, I would never have thought of that. Never in a million years. But that is what I mean about experience and change. Under the colonial system, it doesn't happen. It can't. Of course, the situation on an American Indian reservation is extreme, because a large part of the environment that the American Indian faces are American whites.

Let me now return to the two elements of change, decay of institution and social isolation. When you have peasant people and institutions decay, it looks to me that you just get bigger and better intermediaries, marginal men. When an urban person's institutions decay, and by urban I mean middle-class, he is blocked off from coming true. It gives him identity problems. Institutions for

[17] **aspirations**—desires for high achievement.

him are not so much where he makes decisions about jobs and environment, although that's true, too, but he makes decisions about himself in those institutions. But tribal people—and this is true of a lot of Africans, Asians, and American Indians—who have their structure taken away are in bad shape because they respond to structure. You know, in the beginning, God said, "We are the people who plant corn," or something of that sort. What you are is defined, given. It is defined in ritual. It is defined in interaction. You take away the institutions and tribal people (and I mean this literally, and, believe me, I know, because I come from a conservative tribal background and I went through this) will do whatever is most pleasurable under the circumstances. If they like to drink, they'll drink themselves right into **oblivion**.[18] There are whole American Indian tribes who are just drinking themselves into oblivion. And I don't think that there is any particular psychological trouble unless whites look at that and tell them it's bad. Then there's trouble.

---

[18] **oblivion**—state of complete forgetfulness; "into oblivion" means until they can remember nothing.

QUESTIONS TO CONSIDER

1. According to the author, in his sawmill example, what class of people are created by the hiring practices on reservations?

2. What does the fishhook industry on the Pine Ridge reservation demonstrate about the Indian Bureau's awareness of the culture it was seeking to help? What kind of Sioux would work in this factory?

3. What was the matter with the cattle program the author described? What solution did he suggest?

4. How was the Sac and Fox industry able to work better than the cattle program? What was different about it?

5. What do you think is Robert K. Thomas's main message to the United States Bureau of Indian Affairs and to those responsible for government policy regarding Native people?

Siege at
Wounded Knee

BY MARY CROW DOG (LAKOTA)

In 1890, members of the Ghost Dance religion on the Lakota Sioux
reservation at Pine Ridge, South Dakota, were becoming increasingly
active in their opposition to United States government policy. Fearful
that those gathering for the Ghost Dance might cause a revolt,
cavalry troopers surrounded a group of Lakota Ghost Dancers near
Wounded Knee Creek and attempted to search them for weapons.
A gun discharged, and the soldiers opened fire, killing 146 Lakota
people, many of them women and children. The officer in charge
was later charged with killing innocent people but found not guilty.

Eighty-three years later, in 1973, members of the American
Indian Movement (AIM), a militant civil rights group, returned to
Wounded Knee to resolve a tribal government dispute and to
argue for improvements in Indian legal and human rights. Violence
erupted and a ten-week siege followed. AIM members as well as
law enforcement officials were killed. The story unfolded day by day
in worldwide news coverage. Different sides in the confrontation
disagreed on what happened and why. Mary Crow Dog, one of
200 AIM activists who took part in the protest and siege, provides
her view in this excerpt from her autobiography Lakota Woman.

"Go ahead and make your stand at Wounded Knee."
Wounded Knee, South Dakota, 1973

The Oglala[1] elders thought that we all had been wasting our time and energies in Rapid City and Custer[2] when the knife was at our throats at home. And so, finally and inevitably, our caravan started rolling toward Pine Ridge. [Tribal president Dicky] Wilson was expecting us. His heavily armed goons[3] had been reinforced by a number of rednecks[4] with Remingtons and Winchesters on gun racks behind their driver's seats, eager to bag themselves an Injun.[5] The marshals and FBI had come too, with some thirty armored cars equipped with machine guns and rocket launchers. These were called APCs, Armored Personnel Carriers. The tribal office had been sandbagged and a machine gun installed on its roof. The Indians called it "Fort Wilson." Our movements were kept under observation and reported several times a day. Still we came on.

To tell the truth, I had not joined the caravan with the notion that I would perform what some people later called "that great symbolic act." I did not even know that we would wind up at Wounded Knee. Nobody did.

. . . There was still no definite plan for what to do. We had all assumed that we would go to Pine Ridge town, the administrative center of the reservation, the seat of Wilson's and the government's power. We had always thought that the fate of the Oglalas would be settled there. But as the talks progressed it became clear that nobody wanted us to storm Pine Ridge, **garrisoned**[6] as it was by the goons, the marshals, and the FBI. We did not

---

[1] Oglala—a tribe within the Sioux nation.

[2] Rapid City and Custer—two cities in South Dakota located to the northwest of the Pine Ridge reservation.

[3] goons—thugs hired to intimidate or harm opponents.

[4] rednecks—offensive slang term for the white, rural, laboring class.

[5] Injun—offensive slang term for an Indian.

[6] **garrisoned**—occupied as a military post.

want to be slaughtered. There had been too many massacred Indians already in our history. But if not Pine Ridge, then what? As I remember, it was the older women like Ellen Moves Camp and Gladys Bissonette who first pronounced the magic words "Wounded Knee," who said, "Go ahead and make your stand at Wounded Knee. If you men won't do it, you can stay here and talk for all eternity and we women will do it."

When I heard the words "Wounded Knee" I became very, very serious. Wounded Knee—*Cankpe Opi* in our language—has a special meaning for our people. There is the long ditch into which the frozen bodies of almost three hundred of our people, mostly women and children, were thrown like so much cordwood. And the bodies are still there in their mass grave, unmarked except for a cement border. Next to the ditch, on a hill, stands the white-painted Catholic church, gleaming in the sunlight, the monument of an **alien**[7] faith imposed upon the landscape. And below it flows Cankpe Opi Wakpala, the creek along which the women and children were hunted down like animals by Custer's old Seventh,[8] out to avenge themselves for their defeat by butchering the helpless ones. That happened long ago, but no Sioux ever forgot it.

Wounded Knee is part of our family's history. Leonard's[9] great-grandfather, the first Crow Dog, had been one of the leaders of the Ghost Dancers. He and his group had held out in the icy ravines of the Badlands[10] all winter, but when the soldiers came in force to kill all

---

[7] **alien**—foreign; belonging to another, very different, society.

[8] Custer's old Seventh—In 1876, General George Armstrong Custer and troopers of the Seventh Cavalry units he commanded were killed by Sioux and other Indian warriors at the Battle of Little Bighorn in Montana. In 1890, elements of the same Seventh Cavalry committed the massacre at Wounded Knee, South Dakota.

[9] Leonard's—belonging to Leonard Crow Dog, the author's husband, and the political activist and spiritual leader who led this group to Wounded Knee.

[10] Badlands—a region of rugged, rocky hills and sparse vegetation located in western South Dakota.

the Ghost Dancers he had surrendered his band to avoid having his people killed. Old accounts describe how Crow Dog simply sat down between the rows of soldiers on one side, and the Indians on the other, all ready and eager to start shooting. He had covered himself with a blanket and was just sitting there. Nobody knew what to make of it. The leaders on both sides were so puzzled that they just did not get around to opening fire. They went to Crow Dog, lifted the blanket, and asked him what he meant to do. He told them that sitting there with the blanket over him was the only thing he could think of to make all the hotheads,[11] white and red, curious enough to forget fighting. Then he persuaded his people to lay down their arms. Thus he saved his people just a few miles away from where Big Foot and his band were massacred. And old Uncle Dick Fool Bull, a relative of both the Crow Dogs and my own family, often described to me how he himself heard the rifle and cannon shots that mowed our people down when he was a little boy camping only two miles away. He had seen the bodies, too, and described to me how he had found the body of a dead baby girl with an American flag beaded on her tiny bonnet.

Before we set out for Wounded Knee, Leonard and Wallace Black Elk prayed for all of us with their pipe. I counted some fifty cars full of people. We went right through Pine Ridge. The half-bloods and goons, the marshals and the government snipers on their rooftop, were watching us, expecting us to stop and start a confrontation, but our caravan drove right by them, leaving them wondering. From Pine Ridge it was only eighteen miles more to our destination. Leonard was in the first car and I was way in the back.

Finally, on February 27, 1973, we stood on the hill where the fate of the old Sioux nation, Sitting Bull's and

---

[11] hotheads—quick-tempered people.

Crazy Horse's nation,[12] had been decided, and where we, ourselves, came face to face with our fate. We stood silently, some of us wrapped in our blankets, separated by our personal thoughts and feelings, and yet united, shivering a little with excitement and the chill of a fading winter. You could almost hear our heartbeats.

It was not cold on this next-to-last day of February—not for a South Dakota February anyway. Most of us had not even bothered to wear gloves. I could feel a light wind stirring my hair, blowing it gently about my face. There were a few snowflakes in the air. We all felt the presence of the spirits of those lying close by in the long ditch, wondering whether we were about to join them, wondering when the marshals would arrive. We knew that we would not have to wait long for them to make their appearance.

. . . Suddenly the spell was broken. Everybody got busy. The men were digging trenches and making bunkers, putting up low walls of cinder blocks, establishing a last-resort defense perimeter around the Sacred Heart Church. Those few who had weapons were checking them, mostly small-bore .22s and old hunting rifles. We had only one automatic weapon, an AK-47[13] that one Oklahoma boy had brought back from Vietnam as a souvenir. Altogether we had twenty-six firearms—not much compared to what the other side would bring up against us. None of us had any illusions that we could take over Wounded Knee unopposed. Our message, to the government was: "Come and discuss our demands or kill us!" Somebody called someone on the outside from a telephone inside the trading post. I could hear him yelling proudly again and again, "We hold the Knee!"[14]

---

[12] Sitting Bull's and Crazy Horse's nation—the Dakota Sioux. These two chiefs defeated General George A. Custer at the Battle of Little Bighorn in 1876, the most famous of all Indian victories.

[13] AK-47—Russian-made assault rifle.

[14] The occupiers were besieged by federal marshals until May 8, when AIM surrendered after securing a promise that their complaints would be investigated. Two Indians and one marshal were killed during the fighting.

QUESTIONS TO CONSIDER

1. Why does the author refer to the Sioux tribal office as "Fort Wilson"?

2. Why do you think that tribal leaders on the Pine Ridge reservation opposed the AIM activists?

3. What emotions does Mary Crow Dog feel when the activists decide to go to Wounded Knee?

4. To the activists, why did taking control of Wounded Knee seem like a more effective method of making their point than conducting demonstrations in the towns of Rapid City and Custer?

5. What were the goals of the activists once they reached Wounded Knee?

A Brief History of the American Indian Movement

BY AIM

Established in 1968 in Minneapolis, the American Indian Movement (AIM) is an activist human rights organization. Controversial—even among some Indians—because of its militant tactics, some critics have called AIM radical. In its early years in the 1970s, AIM staged protest events, including sit-ins at the Washington, D.C., offices of the Bureau of Indian Affairs, a nineteen-month Native occupation of federally owned Alcatraz Island in San Francisco Bay, the seizure of a Wisconsin dam, and a seventy-one-day occupation and gun battle with government officials at the site of the historic Wounded Knee massacre in South Dakota. The following excerpts from AIM's Internet website in 1998 explain the organization's spiritual underpinnings and provide a brief history.

In the thirty years of its formal history (the movement existed for 500 years without a name), the American Indian Movement (AIM) has given witness to a great many changes. The leaders and members of today's AIM never fail to remember all of those who have traveled on before, having given their talent and their lives for the survival of the people.

At the core of the movement is Indian leadership under the direction of NeeGawNwayWeeDun, Clyde H. Bellecourt, and others. Making steady progress, the movement has transformed policy-making into programs and organizations that have served Indian people in many communities. These policies have consistently been made in consultation with spiritual leaders and elders. The success of these efforts is indisputable, but perhaps even greater than the accomplishments is the vision defining what AIM stands for.

Indian people were never intended to survive the settlement of Europeans in the Western Hemisphere, our Turtle Island. With the strength of a spiritual base, AIM has been able to clearly **articulate**[1] the claims of Native nations and has had the will and intellect to put forth those claims.

The movement was founded to turn the attention of Indian people toward a renewal of spirituality which would impart the strength of resolve needed to reverse the ruinous policies of the United States, Canada, and other colonialist governments of Central and South America. At the heart of AIM is deep spirituality and a belief in the connectedness of all Indian people.

During the past thirty years, the American Indian Movement has organized communities and created opportunities for people across the Americas and Canada. AIM is headquartered in Minneapolis with chapters in many other cities, rural areas, and Indian nations.

AIM has repeatedly brought successful suit against the federal government for the protection of the rights of Native nations guaranteed in treaties, **sovereignty**,[2] the

---

[1] **articulate**—give voice to.

[2] **sovereignty**—recognized status as a people.

United States Constitution, and laws. The philosophy of **self-determination**[3] upon which the movement is built is deeply rooted in traditional spirituality, culture, language, and history. AIM develops partnerships to address the common needs of the people. Its first **mandate**[4] is to ensure the fulfillment of treaties made with the United States. This is the clear and unwavering vision of the American Indian Movement.

It has not been an easy path. Spiritual leaders and elders foresaw the testing of AIM's strength and stamina. Doubters, **infiltrators**,[5] those who wished they were in the leadership, and those who didn't want to be but wanted to tear down and take away have had their turns. No one, inside or outside the movement, has so far been able to destroy the will and strength of AIM's solidarity. Men and women, adults and children are continuously urged to stay strong spiritually, and to always remember that the movement is greater than the accomplishments or faults of its leaders.

Inherent in the spiritual heart of AIM is knowing that the work goes on because the need goes on. Indian people live on Mother Earth with the clear understanding that no one will assure the coming generations except ourselves. No one from the outside will do this for us. And no person among us can do it all for us, either. Self-determination must be the goal of all work. **Solidarity**[6] must be the first and only defense of the members.

In November, 1972, AIM brought a caravan of Native nation representatives to Washington, D.C., to the place where dealings with Indians have taken place since 1849—the U.S. Department of [the] Interior. AIM

---

[3] **self-determination**—freedom of the people of a given area to determine their own political status; political independence.

[4] **mandate**—command from its members.

[5] **infiltrators**—spies.

[6] **Solidarity**—union of interests and purposes among members of a group.

put the following claims directly before the President of the United States:[7]

from the Trail of Broken Treaties— 20-Point Indian Manifesto

1. Restoration of treaty-making (ended by Congress in 1871).

2. Establishment of a treaty commission to make new treaties (with sovereign Native nations).

3. Indian leaders to address Congress.

4. Review of treaty commitments and violations.

5. Unratified treaties to go before the Senate.

6. All Indians to be governed by treaty relations.

7. Relief for Native nations for treaty rights violations.

8. Recognition of the right of Indians to interpret treaties.

9. Joint congressional committee to be formed on reconstruction[8] of Indian relations.

10. Restoration of 110 million acres of land taken away from Native nations by the United States.

11. Restoration of terminated rights.

12. Repeal of state jurisdiction on Native nations.

13. Federal protection for offenses against Indians.

14. Abolishment of the Bureau of Indian Affairs.[9]

---

[7] President of the United States—Richard M. Nixon (1969–75).

[8] **reconstruction**—re-establishment.

[9] Bureau of Indian Affairs—the agency (BIA) within the Department of the Interior that oversees reservations and relations between the government and Native people.

15. Creation of a new office of Federal Indian Relations.

16. New office to remedy breakdown in the constitutionally prescribed relationships between the United States and Native nations.

17. Native nations to be **immune to**[10] commerce regulation, taxes, [and] trade restrictions of states.

18. Indian religious freedom and cultural integrity protected.

19. Establishment of national Indian voting with local options; free national Indian organizations from governmental controls.

20. Reclaim and affirm health, housing, employment, economic development, and education for all Indian people. . . .

These twenty points, twenty-six years later, state clearly what has to happen if there is to be protection of Native rights, and a future free from the dictates of the country that surrounds the Native nations. These claims clearly reaffirm that Indian people are sovereign people. Despite the history and the accomplishments, AIM is difficult to identify for some people. It seems to stand for many things at once—the protection of treaty rights . . . [as well as] the preservation of spirituality and culture. But what else? Unlike the American civil rights movement, with which it has been compared, AIM has seen self-determination and racism differently. **Desegregation**[11] was not a goal. Individual rights were not placed ahead of the preservation of Native nation sovereignty. At the 1971 AIM national conference it was decided that translating policy to practice meant

---

[10] **immune to**—exempt from.

[11] **Desegregation**—the elimination of laws and customs that required separate schools and other facilities for a specific racial group, such as African Americans.

building organizations—schools and housing and employment services. In Minnesota, AIM's birthplace, that is exactly what was done.

Over the years, as the organizations have grown, they have continued to serve the community from a base of Indian culture. Before AIM in 1968, culture had been weakened in most Indian communities due to U.S. policy, the American boarding schools and all the other efforts to extinguish Indian **secular**[12] and spiritual life. Now, many groups cannot remember a time without culture. This great revival has also helped to restore spiritual leaders and elders to their former positions of **esteem**[13] for the wisdom and the history they hold. All of these actions are in concert with the principles of AIM and came into being at this time in history because Indian people have refused to **relinquish**[14] their sovereign right to exist as free and uncolonized people.

A Chronology

1968
Minneapolis AIM Patrol: created to address issues of extensive police brutality.

1969
Alcatraz Island occupied for nineteen months. AIM was there when United Indians of All Tribes reclaimed federal land in the name of Native nations.

Indian Health Board of Minneapolis founded. This is the first Indian urban-based health care provider in the nation.

---

[12] **secular**—worldly rather than spiritual.

[13] **esteem**—being admired.

[14] **relinquish**—give up.

1970

Legal Rights Center: created to assist in alleviating legal issues facing Indian people. (By 1994, over 19,000 clients have had legal representation.)

1971

Citizen's Arrest of John Old Crow: Takeover of the Bureau of Indian Affairs' main office in Washington, D.C., to show improper BIA policies. Twenty-four arrested for "trespassing" and released. BIA Commissioner Louis Bruce shows his AIM membership card at the meeting held after the release of those arrested.

First National AIM Conference: Eighteen chapters of AIM convened to develop long-range strategy for future directions of the movement.

Takeover of Dam: AIM assists the Lac Court Orieles Ojibwa in Wisconsin in taking over a dam controlled by Northern States Power, which flooded much of the reservation land. This action leads to support by government officials and eventual settlement, returning over 25,000 acres of land to the tribe and actually providing significant monies and business opportunities to the tribe.

1972

Heart of the Earth Survival School: a kindergarten-through-twelfth-grade school established to address the extremely high drop-out rate among American Indian students and lack of cultural programming, it serves as the first model of community-based, student-centered education with culturally correct curriculum operating under parental control.

Trail of Broken Treaties: a march on Washington, D.C., ending in the occupation of BIA headquarters and resulting in the presentation of a twenty-point solution paper to President Nixon.

1973

Legal Action For School Funds: In reaction to the Trail of Broken Treaties, the government abruptly canceled education grants to AIM schools. Through successful legal action, the U.S. District Court orders the grants restored and government payment of costs and attorney fees.

Wounded Knee '73: AIM was contacted by Lakota [Sioux] elders for assistance in dealing with the corruption within the BIA and Tribal Council, which led to the famed seventy-one-day occupation and battle with the U.S. armed forces.

1974

International Indian Treaty Council (IITC): An organization representing Indian peoples throughout the Western Hemisphere [is formed] at the [European headquarters of the] United Nations in Geneva, Switzerland.

Wounded Knee Trials: Eight months of trials in Minneapolis resulted from events which occurred during the 1973 Wounded Knee occupation. In the longest federal trial in the history of the United States, many instances of government misconduct were revealed. U.S. District Judge Fred Nichol dismissed all charges due to government "misconduct" which "formed a pattern throughout the course of the trial" so that "the waters of justice have been polluted."

1975

Federation of Survival Schools: created to provide advocacy and networking skills to sixteen survival schools throughout the U.S. and Canada.

Little Earth of United Tribes: [U.S. Department of Housing and Urban Development] chose AIM to be the prime sponsor of the first Indian-run housing project.

1977

The Longest Walk: Indian nations walk across the U.S. from California to Washington, D.C., to protest anti-Indian legislation calling for the **abrogation**[15] of treaties. A tipi is set up and maintained on the grounds of the White House. The proposed anti-Indian legislation is defeated.

Women of All Red Nations (WARN): established to address issues directly facing Indian women and their families.

1979

Little Earth Housing Protected: an attempt by the U.S. Department of Housing and Urban Development [HUD] to foreclose on the Little Earth of United Tribes housing project is halted by legal action and the U.S. District Court issues an injunction against HUD.

American Indian Opportunities Industrialization Center (AIOIC): creates job training schools to attack the outrageous unemployment issues of Indian people. Over 17,000 Native Americans have been trained for jobs since AIM created the American Indian Opportunities Industrialization Center in 1979.

1986

Schools Lawsuit: AIM schools successfully sue the U.S. Department of Education['s] Indian Education Programs for unfairly ranking the schools' programs below funding recommendation levels. The schools proved bias in the system of ranking by the Department staff.

1989

Spearfishing: AIM is requested to provide expertise in dealing with angry protesters on boat landings. Spearfishing continues despite violence, arrests, and

---

[15] **abrogation**—voiding.

threats from white racists. Senator Daniel Inouye calls for a study on the effects of Indian spearfishing. The study shows only six percent of fish taken are by Indians. Sports fishing accounts for the rest.

1991

Sundance Returned to Minnesota: With the support of the Dakota [Sioux] communities, a great spiritual rebirth took place at Pipestone, Minnesota. Ojibwe nations, too, have helped make the Minnesota Sundance possible. The Pipestone Sundance has since become an annual event.

In 1991, leaders of the Oglala Lakota, Cheyenne and other nations declared independence from the United States. The group established a provisional government and began the other work of developing a separate nation.

National Coalition on Racism in Sports and Media: Organized to address the use of Indians as sports team mascots. AIM led a walk in Minneapolis to the 1992 Superbowl. In 1994, *The Minneapolis Star-Tribune* agreed to stop using professional sports team names that refer to Indian people.

1992

The Food Connection: Organized summer youth jobs program with an organic garden and spiritual camp (Common Ground) at Tonkawood Farm in Orono, Minnesota.

1993

Expansion of American Indian OIC Job-Training Program: The Grand Metropolitan, Inc. of Great Britain, a parent of the Pillsbury Corporation, merges its job-training program with that of AIOIC and pledges future monies and support.

Little Earth: After an eighteen-year struggle, HUD Secretary [Henry] Cisneros rules that [the] Little Earth of United Tribes housing project shall retain the right to Indian preference.

Wounded Knee Anniversary: Gathering for a twentieth anniversary of the Wounded Knee action, Oglala Sioux tribal president thanks AIM for the 1973 actions.

1996

International Encounter for Humanity and Against Neo-Liberalism: Delegates of the International Indian Treaty Council and the American Indian Movement attended meetings hosted by the Emiliano Zapata Liberation Movement (EZLM), held in LaRealidad in the Lancondone Rainforest of Eastern Chiapaz, Mexico.

1998

Twenty-fifth Anniversary of Wounded Knee: an Oglala Lakota nation resolution established February 27th as a National Day of Liberation.

Thirtieth Anniversary of the American Indian Movement. Grand Governing Council; Sacred Pipestone Quarries in Pipestone, Minnesota.

QUESTIONS TO CONSIDER

1. What, according to its leaders, are the guiding principles of AIM?
2. What was the primary thrust of the Trail of Broken Treaties manifesto?
3. What is meant by "self-determination must be the goal" of all AIM's work?
4. How would you characterize the organization's activities listed in the chronology? Principally, what kinds of activities are these? What issues do they address?

Mr. President: Protect the Earth

BY CORBIN HARNEY (SHOSHONE)

Since their first encounters with whites, Native Americans have consistently expressed deep concerns for the welfare of the natural world. Environmental problems in the United States and the rest of the world have provided Indian religious leaders with a more attentive audience than ever before. Corbin Harney, a spiritual leader of the Western Shoshone of Nevada, has spoken out on environmental issues for more than forty years. The fact that the homeland of his people lies near nuclear weapons testing sites has clearly heightened his sense of urgency. After traveling to the former Soviet Union to view the effects of nuclear contamination, his plea to the president of the United States expresses a deep concern for all of the people of the earth.

October 18, 1993
President Bill Clinton
The White House
Washington, D.C.

Dear Mr. President,

I was in Washington for a week at the beginning of October, and I am sorry that I could not meet with you personally, "the White Chief,"[1] about the serious effects of nuclear testing and the radiation that is destroying our Mother Earth.

Coming to Washington was an important part of my work to stop nuclear testing. I met with a number of government officials—with congressmen and senators, officials from the Department of Energy regarding cleanup of the test site in Nevada, peace groups, people against plutonium[2] **proliferation**,[3] and also a talk with the Chinese ambassador . . . on the morning of October 4, the same day they exploded their bomb.

As spiritual leader of the Western Shoshone nation, I want you to understand how nuclear testing and nuclear waste affects not only our people on native lands, but all living things on the earth.

The whole world is quickly becoming contaminated. As I see it, time is very short, and everything on the planet today is suffering. The water, air, and Mother Earth herself are beginning to die from the effects of nuclear power. What good will our world be in a few years if we are all suffering from the effects of nuclear radiation?

I have traveled to Kazakhstan[4] and witnessed some very sad things. They cannot use their water any more

[1] "the White Chief"—Indian term for the president of the United States.

[2] plutonium—a radioactive element used in making nuclear weapons.

[3] **proliferation**—rapid spread or growth.

[4] Kazakhstan—country in central Asia. Until 1990, Kazakhstan was part of the Soviet Union and was used to store large amounts of nuclear weapons and plutonium.

due to contamination. A few years ago, the water spoke to me: "I'm going to look like water, but pretty soon no one is going to be able to use me." You may not realize it, but time is running out for the rest of us, too—all over the world.

I have seen the effects of nuclear radiation, both in our country among the "down-winders"[5] and in Kazakhstan: children being born with eyes over their ears, arms coming out of their sides, and many other birth defects, as well as leukemia and cancers among the adults after only a short time.

As human beings, we have broken our connection with our Mother Earth. All the food that our people have relied upon for thousands of years is beginning to die out. The berries and native plants are gone; the plants don't grow strong like they used to; and the water is becoming contaminated all over the planet. Even our traditional medicine plants are not growing as they should, and are disappearing.

Our native ceremonies recognize our connection to the earth. We know that everything out there—all the living things: the trees, the plants, even the rocks—everything is conscious. Our Mother Earth is a living, conscious being. When all the people of the world realize this—that all living things need and use the same water, the same air— then we can begin to change our relationship to the earth. We have to bring this consciousness back to the people, and lead the people back to nature.

A long time ago our ancestors told us that some day the people would look to the Indian to lead us in the right direction. We came to Washington to work together with the people [who] run the government, because we are all in this mess together. I am not a scientist or nuclear physicist, nor can I solve the technical and very complex problem of how to deal with nuclear contamination.

---

[5] "down-winders"—people who live within an area of potential nuclear contamination; "down wind" is in the direction toward which the wind blows.

I do know that we have to unite all the people of the earth, begin an honest **dialogue**[6] of what has happened already, and work together to help save the earth. The earth is not an object for us to manipulate, but a living being that gives all of us life.

We pray to protect the land, and all living things out there. The spirit of the land has said to me that we're going to have to help her out. If we don't protect the land, our Mother Earth is going to suffer even more in the very near future.

We know that all people, no matter where they live, are natives of Mother Earth. We only have one water and one air that we all drink and breathe. You can help all of us by deciding not to contaminate the earth any further. We encourage you, Mr. President, to stand up and be strong in your decision to protect the earth.

Your decision not to continue testing[7]—despite what the Chinese or French might do, and despite British urgings—will send a strong message to the other countries who are not so wise or conscious. Remember that this pollution and contamination is already spreading all over the earth, and our water is becoming radioactive.

I am speaking to you for all the people of the earth, and for all living things. I hope you will listen to me very carefully, take into your heart what I am saying, and then take all the right actions to help save our Mother Earth.

Sincerely,
Corbin Harney
Spiritual Leader of the Western Shoshone Nation

---

[6] **dialogue**—conversation.

[7] continue testing—continue to explode new nuclear weapons in tests to see if they work.

QUESTIONS TO CONSIDER

1. What does the author mean when he says that people have broken their connection to the earth?

2. How has the author's letter affected your perspective on Native American religious beliefs?

3. In your opinion, how effective is this letter to President Clinton?

On Columbus's Quincentennial

BY N. SCOTT MOMADAY (KIOWA)

The year 1992 was met with deeply mixed feelings by many Native Americans. The 500th anniversary of Christopher Columbus's first voyage and "discovery" of America was also seen as the date that white men in ever-increasing numbers began arriving in the Western Hemisphere, pushing out the Indian inhabitants and destroying their cultures and religion. At least one leader demanded that Columbus Day be redesignated as a national day of mourning. Pulitzer Prize-winning novelist and poet N. Scott Momaday—the son of a Kiowa father and a part-Cherokee mother—reflects in this essay on the Columbus celebration in the United States and sees 1492 as a time when "the whole history of Europe" bore down on a new continent, whose inhabitants "couldn't imagine what was coming upon their shore." Momaday won the Pulitzer Prize in 1968 for his second book, House Made of Dawn, *which describes a Native American veteran of World War II struggling to recover his spirit in the white man's world.*

I've done some thinking on Columbus. I'm very much interested in the significance of the occasion. I think that it's a wonderfully important time to reflect over the meaning of Columbus's voyages to America, and the following establishment of colonial settlements in the world. The whole history of Indian/white relations from 1492 to the present is a large subject to get at, but is **eminently**[1] worth thinking about. I would hope that the question would produce greater awareness of Native cultures, the importance of those cultures, and indeed the **indispensable**[2] importance of them in the light of the twenty-first century.

I think we're on the brink of disaster on many fronts. I believe that the Native people can help us out of that, help push us back away from that brink. At one time I was more optimistic than I am now, but I think that we have to operate on hope, that it is possible to reverse this march toward **annihilation**[3] that we have begun on the nuclear front and on the **ecological**[4] front. I think that the Native American broad experience of the environment in the Americas is an important research resource for us.

I just returned from Europe, and I talked to a good many people there who seem to be more keenly aware of ecological problems than we are here. We're very comfortable. We have committed ourselves to a technological society in such a way that it is hard for us to see anything outside that context. So it's very hard for us to understand that we are polluting the atmosphere. We know we are, but we have the tendency to think that we are so intelligent as a people and we have achieved such a high degree of civilization that the solutions will come about in the course of time. That's a dangerous attitude.

---

[1] **eminently**—to an outstanding degree.

[2] **indispensable**—invaluable; impossible to do without.

[3] **annihilation**—total destruction.

[4] **ecological**—environmental.

I think Native people are receiving information about this just as the rest of us are. Native people seem to live harmoniously with the physical world as it is, and so I think that the dangers of pollution are more keenly felt outside the Native American world than in it. Native Americans need to be as informed as the rest of us, because they probably have more solutions.

I think we're at a crucial point with youth not learning traditions. In the sixties and seventies, for example, there was a great concern among Native Americans to preserve cultural values and young people were anxious to learn the traditional ways. I'm no longer so sure that those values are being maintained. I hope they are, but I can't feel as confident about it as I was, say ten years ago. I would like to be in a position where I observe more closely what is going on with Indian people.

I have done three large paintings, acrylic on canvas, of what I call the Columbian **triad**.[5] Each of these is a portrait of Columbus. One is a skeletal, skull-like portrait with a mermaid above it, titled "Admiral of the Ocean," and then there is one of a dark full-face portrait called "Palos," which is the port from which Columbus set sail. The third one is "San Salvador," a depiction of Columbus in a full figure adjacent to an Indian child. Columbus is an emaciated, death-like figure, and the child is pure, innocent, small, and naked. It's a confrontation of the old world and the new world.

I was thinking about what his discovery meant finally, in the long run. Of course it is hard to say, but certainly one valid aspect is the complete revolution in the Americas. When Columbus came to the Americas, apparently he was very **benevolent**[6] to the Indians, as they were to him, but there followed a clash of cultures which worked against the Indians and destroyed their culture. I wanted to represent Columbus as an unwitting

---

[5] **triad**—group of three (images).

[6] **benevolent**—kind and fair.

threat to the culture, and that was reenacted many, many times in many places. And that's what I point to in the irony of the confrontation. Columbus had no idea where he was. He died believing he had been to China.

I have mixed feelings about celebrating this event which was certainly, from some perspectives, tragic. . . . I had similar feelings in 1976 at the Bicentennial of the Constitution.[7] I had a hard time with that, as a Native American, knowing that there was no reason whatsoever to celebrate the 200th anniversary but, on the other hand, I felt that was a fairly narrow attitude. Indians just as much as anyone else have the right to celebrate the occasion. I think if Indians exclude themselves from it, that's a negative thing. If they can find a way to celebrate it on a real basis, that's positive. They have come to an interesting and crucial point in their history. They stand to teach the rest of the world that there's something good about celebration.

It's very hard to be specific about how to change the future. The major issues we face now are survival—how to live in the modern world. Part of that is how to remain Indian, how to assimilate without ceasing to be an Indian. I think some important strides have been made. Indians remain Indian, and against pretty good odds. They remain Indian and, in some situations, by a thread. Their languages are being lost at a tremendous rate, poverty is rampant, as is alcoholism. But still there are Indians, and the traditional world is still intact.

It's a matter of identity. It's thinking about who I am. I grew up on Indian reservations, and then I went away from the Indian world and entered a different context. But I continue to think of myself as Indian, I write out of

---

[7] Bicentennial of the Constitution—The author is referring to the 200th anniversary of the Declaration of Independence. The bicentennial of the Constitution did not occur until 1989.

that conviction. I think this is what most Indian people are doing today. They go off the reservations, but they keep an idea of themselves as Indians. That's the trick.

I have been asked, how do you define an Indian, is it a matter of blood content? I say no, an Indian is someone who thinks of themselves as an Indian. But that's not so easy to do and one has to earn the entitlement somehow. You have to have a certain experience of the world in order to formulate this idea. I know how my father saw the world, and his father before him. That's how I see the world.

QUESTIONS TO CONSIDER

1. What are the mixed feelings that Momaday has about Native Americans celebrating the 500th anniversary of Columbus's voyage in 1492?

2. What would you say Momaday describes as the Indian's place in America?

3. Why does Momaday think Native cultures will be so vitally important to the world in the twenty-first century?

The Battle of Wounded Knee On December 29, 1890, 300 Sioux Indians were massacred at Wounded Knee Creek, South Dakota, as the United States Army tried to arrest Sioux Chief Big Foot. In this last major battle in the Indian Wars, the chief was slain along with his people. The battle also marked the end of the Ghost Dance movement that had given hope to Native peoples who wanted to salvage their traditional way of life.

Culture Clash

Background Battle of Wounded Knee.

Body of Big Foot. ▶

On February 27, 1973, a group called the American Indian Movement (AIM) seized control of Wounded Knee. Led by AIM leader Russell Means, the occupation began as a protest against the reservation's officially sanctioned government. Three people were killed during the seventy-one-day occupation, twelve were wounded, and nearly 1,200 were arrested.

THE *Spirit* of the past will Rise to claim the FUTURE

WOUNDED KNEE.

IN THE MOON WHEN THE DEER SHED THEIR HORNS (DEC. 28, 1890)

MARCH 1973...

AIM leaders.
▼

Troops block the street.
▼

UNDED KNEE → 7 Mi
NDERSON → 16 Mi
RCUPINE → 15 Mi
CKYFORD → 38 Mi
ENIC → 56 Mi
LE → 42 Mi

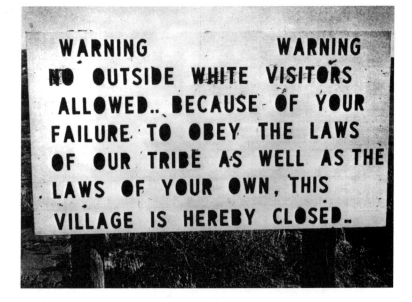

▲

Sign of the Times This sign warns tourists not to enter Old Oraibi, a Hopi community in Arizona. Oraibi is one of the two oldest continuously inhabited settlements in North America. Tourists were banned from the community after they failed to respect rules against photographing sacred Hopi dances.

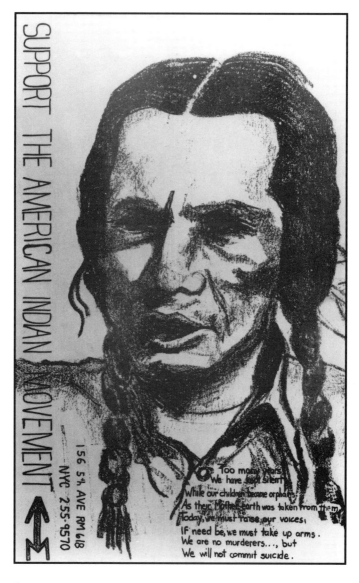

This poster advises people to support the American Indian Movement, a group whose activities on behalf of Native Americans were inspired by the African-American Civil Rights Movement.

▲

A tipi is erected outside the White House in 1978 as part of a protest for Native American rights.

▲

President Bill Clinton watches a ceremony being performed during a meeting
with Native American leaders at the White House.

ACKNOWLEDGEMENTS

Texts

12 From "Prophesies of Our Grandparents" in *The Zunis Self-Portrayals* by The Zuni People, translated by Alvina Quam. Reprinted by permission of the Zuni People.

17 "The First Ship" from *American Indian Myths and Legends* by Richard Erdoes and Alfonso Ortiz, editors. Copyright © 1984 by Richard Erdoes and Alfonso Ortiz. Reprinted by permission of Pantheon Books, a division of Random House, Inc.

20 From *Cheyenne Memories* by John Stands In Timber and Margot Liberty. Copyright © 1967 by Yale University. Reprinted by permission of Yale University Press, publisher.

36 From "The Code of Handsome Lake" by Chief Jacob Thomas from *Teachings From The Longhouse* by Chief Jacob Thomas and Terry Boyle. Reprinted by permission of Stoddart Publishing Co. Limited.

44 From "Janitin Is Named Jesús" "Testimonio de Janitil" from *Apuntes Historicos de la Baja California* by Manuel C. Roja, Bancroft Library (Mss. #295). Reprinted by permission.

128 "Recollections of Removal" by Rebecca Neugin from *Indian Removal: The Emigration of the Five Civilized Tribes of the Indians,* by Grant Foreman. Copyright 1932 and 1953 by the University of Oklahoma Press, Norman. Reprinted by permission.

136 "The Nez Perces Indians" by James Reuben as appeared in *The Chronicles of Oklahoma,* Vol. 12, September, 1934. Copyright 1934; Reprinted by permission from The Chronicles of Oklahoma (Oklahoma City: Oklahoma Historical Society, 1934).

146 Condensed and adapted from "The Line" in *Me and Mine: The Life Story of Helen Sekaquaptewa,* as told to Louise Udall. Copyright © 1969 The Arizona Board of Regents. Reprinted by permission of the University of Arizona Press.

152 "We Missed the Bus" by George Peequaquat as appeared in *Voices Under One Sky* by Trish Fox Roman. Reprinted by permission of George Peequaquat.

166 Interview with Alfred DuBray, American Indian Research Project #533 and interview with Ramon Roubideaux, American Indian Research Project #6, preserved by the Oral History Center, Institute for Indian Studies, University of South Dakota, Vermillion, SD 57069, as appeared in *To Be an Indian: An Oral History* edited by Joseph H. Cash and Herbert T. Hoover. Reprinted by permission of Herbert T. Hoover.

173 "A New Arrival, 1968" from *Division Street: America* by Studs Terkel. Reprinted by permission of Donadio & Olson, Inc. Copyright 1967 by Studs Terkel.

173 From "Benny Bearskin, 45" from *Division Street: America* by Studs Terkel. Reprinted by permission of Donadio & Olson, Inc. Copyright 1967 by Studs Terkel.

178 "On An Indian Reservation: How Colonialism Works" from "Colonialism: Classic and Internal," by Robert K. Thomas, *New University* Thought, Vol. IV, No. 4, Winter, 1966–7, pp. 39–43.

187 From "Cankpe Opi Wakpala" from *Lakota Woman* by Mary Crow Dog with Richard Erdoes. Copyright © 1990 by Mary Crow Dog and Richard Erdoes. Used by permission of Grove/Atlantic, Inc.

193 "A Brief History of the American Indian Movement." Adapted from http://alt.sunday.net/html.

204 "Mr. President: Protect the Earth" from *The Way It Is* by Corbin Harney. © 1995 Corbin Harney. Reprinted by permission of Blue Dolphin Publishing, Inc., P.O. Box 8, Nevada City, CA 95959.

209 "Confronting Columbus Again" by N. Scott Momaday as appeared in *Native American Testimony* edited by Peter Nabokov. Copyright © N. Scott Momaday. Reprinted by permission.

Images:

Photo Research Diane Hamilton

25, 29 *top,* **30, 33** *top,* **68** *bottom,* **110, 115** *top,* **116, 163** *bottom* © The Granger Collection

26–28, 29 *bottom,* **31–32, 67, 68** *top,* **70, 111–114, 115** *bottom,* **155–162, 163** *top,* **214–216, 218–220** Courtesy Library of Congress.

33 *bottom* ©Archive Photos/Fred G. Korth

69 © N. Carter/North Wind Picture Archives

217 © Archive Photos/AFP

221 © AP/Wide World Photos

Every effort has been made to secure complete rights and permissions for each selection presented herein. Updated acknowledgements, if needed, will appear in subsequent printings.

Index